THE THEORY OF THE NOVEL

By the same author

THE HISTORICAL NOVEL
THE MEANING OF CONTEMPORARY REALISM
ESSAYS ON THOMAS MANN
GOETHE AND HIS AGE
HISTORY AND CLASS CONSCIOUSNESS
WRITER AND CRITIC
SOLZHENITSYN

The Theory
of the
Novel

A historico-philosophical essay on the forms of great epic literature

by

GEORG LUKÁCS

TRANSLATED FROM THE GERMAN BY
ANNA BOSTOCK

MERLIN PRESS
LONDON

© Hermann Luchterhand Verlag GmbH 1963

Translation © The Merlin Press 1971

First published by P. Cassirer, Berlin, 1920
This edition first published by
The Merlin Press Ltd.,
11 Fitzroy Square, London W.1.
and printed by
Bristol Typesetting Co. Ltd., Barton Manor, Bristol

TRANSLATOR'S NOTE

I should like to acknowledge my debt to Jean Clairevoye, the translator of this book into French (*La Théorie du roman*, Editions Gonthier, Geneva 1963), whose version I consulted at all stages of my work.

A.B.

Contents

Preface

THE FIRST draft of this study was written in the summer of 1914 and the final version in the winter of 1914-15. It first appeared in Max Dessoir's *Zeitschrift für Aesthetik und Allgemeine Kunstwissenschaft* in 1916 and was published in book form by P. Cassirer, Berlin, in 1920.

The immediate motive for writing was supplied by the outbreak of the First World War and the effect which its acclamation by the social-democratic parties had upon the European left. My own deeply personal attitude was one of vehement, global and, especially at the beginning, scarcely articulate rejection of the war and especially of enthusiasm for the war. I recall a conversation with Frau Marianne Weber in the late autumn of 1914. She wanted to challenge my attitude by telling me of individual, concrete acts of heroism. My only reply was: 'The better the worse!' When I tried at this time to put my emotional attitude into conscious terms, I arrived at more or less the following formulation: the Central Powers would probably defeat Russia; this might lead to the downfall of Tsarism; I had no objection to that. There was also some probability that the West would defeat Germany; if this led to the downfall of the Hohenzollerns and the Hapsburgs, I was once again in favour. But then the question arose: who was to save us from Western civilisation? (The prospect of final victory by the Germany of that time was to me nightmarish.)

Such was the mood in which the first draft of *The Theory of the Novel* was written. At first it was meant to take the form of a series of dialogues: a group of young people withdraw from the war psychosis of their environment, just as the story-tellers of the *Decameron* had withdrawn from the, plague; they try to understand themselves and one another by means of conversations which gradually lead to the problems discussed in the book—the outlook on a Dostoevskian world. On closer consideration I dropped this plan and wrote the book as it stands today. Thus it was written in a mood of permanent despair over the state of the world. It was not until 1917 that I found an answer to the problems which, until then, had seemed to me insoluble.

Of course it would be possible to consider this study simply in itself, only from the viewpoint of its objective content, and without reference to the inner factors which conditioned it. But I believe that in looking back over the history of almost five decades it is worth while to describe the mood in which the work was written because this will facilitate a proper understanding of it.

Clearly my rejection of the war and, together with it, of the bourgeois society of that time was purely utopian; nothing, even at the level of the most abstract intellection, helped to mediate between my subjective attitude and objective reality. Methodologically, this had the very important consequence that I did not, at first, feel any need to submit my view of the world, my scientific working method, etc., to critical reassessment. I was then in process of turning from Kant to Hegel, without, however, changing any aspect of my attitude towards the so-called 'intellectual sciences' school, an attitude based essentially on my youthful enthusiasm for the work of Dilthey, Simmel and Max Weber. *The Theory of the Novel* is in effect a typical product of the tendencies of that school. When I met Max Dvorak personally in Vienna in 1920 he told me that he regarded my book as the movement's most important publication.

Today it is no longer difficult to see the limitations of this method. But we are also in a position to appreciate the features which, to a certain extent, justified it historically as against the petty two-dimensionality of Neo-Kantian (or any other) positivism in the treatment both of historical characters or relations and of intellectual realities (logic, aesthetics, etc.). I am thinking, for example, of the fascination exercised by Dilthey's *Das Erlebnis und die Dichtung*[1] (Leipzig 1905), a book which seemed in many respects to open up new ground. This new ground appeared to us then as an intellectual world of large-scale syntheses in both the theoretical and the historical fields. We failed to see that the new method had in fact scarcely succeeded in surmounting positivism, or that its syntheses were without objective foundation. (At that time it escaped the notice of the younger ones among us that men of talent were arriving at their genuinely sound conclusions in spite of the method rather than by means of it.) It became the fashion to form general synthetic concepts on the basis of only a few characteristics—in most cases only intuitively grasped—of a school, a period, etc., then to proceed by deduction from these generalisations to the analysis of individual phenomena, and in that way to arrive at what we claimed to be a comprehensive overall view.

This was the method of *The Theory of the Novel*. Let me quote just a few examples. Its typology of novel forms depends to a large extent on whether the chief protagonist's soul is 'too narrow' or 'too broad' in relation to reality. This highly abstract criterion is useful, at most, for illuminating certain aspects of *Don Quixote*, which is chosen to represent the first type. But it is far too general to afford full comprehension of the historical and aesthetic richness of even that one novel. As for the other novelists placed in the same category, such as Balzac or even Pontoppidan, the method puts them into a conceptual straitjacket which completely distorts them. The same is true of the other types. The consequence of the abstract synthesising practised by

[1] 'Lived Experience and Literary Creation' (trans.)

13

the 'intellectual sciences' school is even more striking in the treatment of Tolstoy. The epilogue in *War and Peace* is, in fact, an authentic conclusion, in terms of ideas, to the period of the Napoleonic Wars; the development of certain figures already foreshadows the Decembrist rising of 1825. But the author of *The Theory of the Novel* sticks so obstinately to the schema of *L'Education sentimentale* that all he can find here is 'a nursery atmosphere where all passion has been spent', 'more melancholy than the ending of the most problematic of novels of disillusionment'. Any number of such examples could be supplied. Suffice it to point out that novelists such as Defoe, Fielding and Stendhal found no place in this schematic pattern, that the arbitrary 'synthetic' method of the author of *The Theory of the Novel* leads him to a completely upside-down view of Balzac and Flaubert or of Tolstoy and Dostoevsky, etc., etc.

Such distortions must be mentioned, if only to reveal the limitations of the method of abstract synthesis practised by the 'intellectual sciences' school. That does not mean, of course, that the author of *The Theory of the Novel* was precluded in principle from uncovering any interesting correlations. Here again I will give only the most characteristic example: the analysis of the role of time in *L'Education sentimentale*. The analysis of the concrete work is still an inadequate abstraction. The discovery of a '*recherche du temps perdu*' can be objectively justified, if at all, only with regard to the last part of the novel (after the final defeat of the revolution of 1848). Nevertheless we have here an unambiguous formulation of the new function of time in the novel, based on the Bergsonian concept of '*durée*'. This is the more striking as Proust did not become known in Germany until after 1920, Joyce's *Ulysses* not until 1922, and Thomas Mann's *The Magic Mountain* was not published until 1924.

Thus *The Theory of the Novel* is a typical product of

'intellectual science' and does not point the way beyond its methodological limitations. Yet its success (Thomas Mann and Max Weber were among those who read it with approval) was not purely accidental. Although rooted in the 'intellectual sciences' approach, this book shows, within the given limitations, certain new features which were to acquire significance in the light of later developments. We have already pointed out that the author of *The Theory of the Novel* had become a Hegelian. The older leading representatives of the 'intellectual sciences' method based themselves on Kantian philosophy and were not free from traces of positivism; this was particularly true of Dilthey. An attempt to overcome the flat rationalism of the positivists nearly always meant a step in the direction of irrationalism; this applies especially to Simmel, but also to Dilthey himself. It is true that the Hegelian revival had already begun several years before the outbreak of the war. But whatever was of serious scientific interest in that revival was largely confined to the sphere of logic or of the general theory of science. So far as I am aware, *The Theory of the Novel* was the first work belonging to the 'intellectual sciences' school in which the findings of Hegelian philosophy were concretely applied to aesthetic problems. The first, general part of the book is essentially determined by Hegel, e.g. the comparison of modes of totality in epic and dramatic art, the historico-philosophical view of what the epic and the novel have in common and of what differentiates them, etc. But the author of *The Theory of the Novel* was not an exclusive or orthodox Hegelian; Goethe's and Schiller's analyses, certain conceptions of Goethe's in his late period (e.g. the demonic), the young Friedrich Schlegel's and Solger's aesthetic theories (irony as a modern method of form-giving), fill out and concretise the general Hegelian outline.

Perhaps a still more important legacy of Hegel is the historicisation of aesthetic categories. In the sphere of aesthetics, this is where the return to Hegel yielded its most useful results. Kantians such as Rickert and his school put a methodological chasm between timeless value and historical realisation of value. Dilthey himself saw the contradiction as far less extreme, but did not (in his preliminary sketches for a method of a history of philosophy) get beyond establishing a meta-historical typology of philosophies, which then achieve historical realisation in concrete variations. He succeeds in this in some of his aesthetic analyses, but, in a sense, he does so *per nefas* and is certainly not aware of inventing a new method. The world-view at the root of such philosophical conservatism is the historico-politically conservative attitude of the leading representatives of the 'intellectual sciences'. Intellectually this attitude goes back to Ranke and is thus in sharp contradiction to Hegel's view of the dialectical evolution of the world spirit. Of course there is also the positivist historical relativism, and it was precisely during the war that Spengler combined this with tendencies of the 'intellectual sciences' school by radically historicising all categories and refusing to recognise the existence of any suprahistorical validity, whether aesthetic, ethical or logical. Yet by doing so he, in turn, abolished the unity of the historical process: his extreme historical dynamism finally became transformed into a static view, an ultimate abolition of history itself, a succession of completely disconnected cultural cycles which always end and always start again. Thus with Spengler we arrive at a secessionist counterpart to Ranke.

The author of *The Theory of the Novel* did not go so far as that. He was looking for a general dialectic of literary *genres* that was based upon the essential nature of aesthetic categories and literary forms, and aspiring to a more intimate connection between category and history than he found in Hegel himself; he strove towards intellectual comprehension of permanence within change and of inner change within the enduring validity of the essence. But his method remains

16

extremely abstract in many respects, including certain matters of great importance; it is cut off from concrete socio-historical realities. For that reason, as has already been pointed out, it leads only too often to arbitrary intellectual constructs. It was not until a decade and a half later (by that time, of course, on Marxist ground) that I succeeded in finding a way towards a solution. When M. A. Lifshitz and I, in opposition to the vulgar sociology of a variety of schools during the Stalin period, were trying to uncover Marx's real aesthetic and to develop it further, we arrived at a genuine historico-systematic method. *The Theory of the Novel* remained at the level of an attempt which failed both in design and in execution, but which in its intention came closer to the right solution than its contemporaries were able to do.

The book's aesthetic problematic of the present is also part of the Hegelian legacy: I mean the notion that development from the historico-philosophical viewpoint leads to a kind of abolition of those aesthetic principles which had determined development up to that point. In Hegel himself, however, only art is rendered problematic as a result of this; the 'world of prose', as he aesthetically defines this condition, is one in which the spirit has attained itself both in thought and in social and state praxis. Thus art becomes problematic precisely because reality has become non-problematic. The idea put forward in *The Theory of the Novel*, although formally similar, is in fact the complete opposite of this: the problems of the novel form are here the mirror-image of a world gone out of joint. This is why the 'prose' of life is here only a symptom, among many others, of the fact that reality no longer constitutes a favourable soil for art; that is why the central problem of the novel is the fact that art has to write off the closed and total forms which stem from a rounded totality of being—that art has nothing more to do with any world of forms that is immanently complete in itself. And this is not for artistic but for historico-philosophical reasons:

'there is no longer any spontaneous totality of being', the author of *The Theory of the Novel* says of present-day reality. A few years later Gottfried Benn put the same thought in another way: '. . . there was no reality, only, at most, its distorted image'.[2] Although *The Theory of the Novel* is, in the ontological sense, more critical and more thoughtful than the expressionist poet's view, the fact nevertheless remains that both were expressing similar feelings about life and reacting to the present in a similar way. During the debate between expressionism and realism in the 1930s, this gave rise to a somewhat grotesque situation in which Ernst Bloch invoked *The Theory of the Novel* in his polemic against the Marxist, Georg Lukács.

It is perfectly evident that the contradiction between *The Theory of the Novel* and Hegel, who was its general methodological guide, is primarily social rather than aesthetic or philosophical in nature. It may suffice to recall what has already been said about the author's attitude towards the war. We should add that his conception of social reality was at that time strongly influenced by Sorel. That is why the present in *The Theory of the Novel* is not defined in Hegelian terms but rather by Fichte's formulation, as 'the age of absolute sinfulness'. This ethically-tinged pessimism vis-à-vis the present does not, however, signify a general turning back from Hegel to Fichte, but, rather, a 'Kierkegaardisation' of the Hegelian dialectic of history. Kierkegaard always played an important role for the author of *The Theory of the Novel*, who, long before Kierkegaard had become fashionable, wrote an essay on the relationship between his life and thought.[3] And during his Heidelberg years immediately

---

[2] From: *Bekenntnis zum Expressionismus* (Expressionist Profession of Faith), in: *Deutsche Zukunft*, 5.11.1933, and *Gesammelte Werke,* ed. D. Wellershoff, Vol. 1, Wiesbaden 1959, p. 245.

[3] *Das Zerschellen der Form am Leben.* (The Shattering of Form against Life.) Written in 1909. Published in German in: *Die Seele und die Formen,* Berlin 1911.

before the war he had been engaged in a study, never to be completed, of Kierkegaard's critique of Hegel. These facts are mentioned here, not for biographical reasons, but to indicate a trend which was later to become important in German thought. It is true that Kierkegaard's direct influence leads to Heidegger's and Jaspers' philosophy of existence and, therefore, to more or less open opposition to Hegel. But it should not be forgotten that the Hegelian revival itself was strenuously concerned with narrowing the gap between Hegel and irrationalism. This tendency is already detectable in Dilthey's researches into the young Hegel (1905) and assumes clearly-defined form in Kroner's statement that Hegel was the greatest irrationalist in the history of philosophy (1924). Kierkegaard's direct influence cannot yet be proved here. But in the 1920s it was present everwhere, in a latent form but to an increasing degree, and even led to a Kierkegaardisation of the young Marx. For example, Karl Löwith wrote in 1941: 'Far as they are from one another (Marx and Kierkegaard, G.L.), they are nevertheless closely connected by their common attack on existing reality and by the fact that both stem from Hegel'. (It is hardly necessary to point out how widespread this tendency is in present-day French philosophy.)

The socio-philosophical basis of such theories is the philosophically as well as politically uncertain attitude of romantic anti-capitalism. Originally, say in the young Carlyle or in Cobbett, this was a genuine critique of the horrors and barbarities of early capitalism—sometimes even, as in Carlyle's *Past and Present*, a preliminary form of a socialist critique. In Germany this attitude gradually transformed itself into a form of apology for the political and social backwardness of the Hohenzollern empire. Viewed superficially, a wartime work as important as Thomas Mann's *Betrachtungen eines Unpolitischen*[4] (1918) belongs to the same tendency. But

[4] 'Meditations of an Unpolitical Man' (trans.)

Thomas Mann's later development, as early as in the 1920s, justifies his own description of this work: 'It is a retreating action fought in the grand manner, the last and latest stand of a German romantic bourgeois mentality, a battle fought with full awareness of its hopelessness . . . even with insight into the spiritual unhealthiness and immorality of any sympathy with that which is doomed to death'.

No trace of such a mood is to be found in the author of *The Theory of the Novel*, for all that his philosophical starting-point was provided by Hegel, Goethe and Romanticism. His opposition to the barbarity of capitalism allowed no room for any sympathy such as that felt by Thomas Mann for the 'German wretchedness' or its surviving features in the present.

The Theory of the Novel is not conservative but subversive in nature, even if based on a highly naïve and totally unfounded utopianism—the hope that a natural life worthy of man can spring from the disintegration of capitalism and the destruction, seen as identical with that disintegration, of the lifeless and life-denying social and economic categories. The fact that the book culminates in its analysis of Tolstoy, as well as the author's view of Dostoevsky, who, it is claimed, 'did not write novels', clearly indicate that the author was not looking for a new literary form but, quite explicitly, for a 'new world'. We have every right to smile at such primitive utopianism, but it expresses nonetheless an intellectual tendency which was part of the reality of that time.

In the twenties, it is true, attempts to reach beyond the economic world by social means acquired an increasingly pronounced reactionary character. But at the time when *The Theory of the Novel* was written these ideas were still in a completely undifferentiated, germinal phase. If Hilferding, the most celebrated economist of the Second International, could write of communist society in his *Finanzkapital*[5] (1909):

---

[5] 'Finance Capital' (trans.)

'Exchange (in such a society: trans.) is accidental, not a possible subject for theoretical economic consideration. It cannot be theoretically analysed, but only psychologically understood'; if we think of the utopias, intended to be revolutionary, of the last war years and the immediate post-war period—then we can arrive at a historically juster assessment of the utopia of *The Theory of the Novel*, without in any way modifying our critical attitude towards its lack of theoretical principle.

Such a critical attitude is particularly well suited to enable us to see in its true light a further peculiarity of *The Theory of the Novel*, which made it something new in German literature. (The phenomenon we are about to examine was known much earlier in France.) To put it briefly, the author of *The Theory of the Novel* had a conception of the world which aimed at a fusion of 'left' ethics and 'right' epistemology (ontology, etc.). In so far as Wilhelminian Germany had any principled oppositional literature at all, this literature was based on the traditions of the Enlightenment (in most cases, moreover, on the most shallow epigones of that tradition) and took a globally negative view of Germany's valuable literary and theoretical traditions. (The socialist Franz Mehring constitutes a rare example in that respect.) So far as I am able to judge, *The Theory of the Novel* was the first German book in which a left ethic oriented towards radical revolution was coupled with a traditional-conventional exegesis of reality. From the 1920s onwards this view was to play an increasingly important role. We need only think of Ernst Bloch's *Der Geist der Utopie*[6] (1918, 1925) and *Thomas Münzer als Theologe der Revolution*[7], of Walter Benjamin, even of the beginnings of Theodor W. Adorno, etc.

The importance of this movement became even greater

[6] 'The Spirit of Utopia' (trans.)
[7] 'Thomas Münzer as the Theologian of Revolution' (trans.)

proceeding from a 'left' ethic, attempted to mobilise Nietzsche and even Bismarck as progressive forces against fascist reaction. (Let me mention in passing that France, where this tendency emerged much earlier than in Germany, today possesses an extremely influential representative of it in the person of J.-P. Sartre. For obvious reasons, the social causes of the earlier appearance and more prolonged effectiveness of this phenomenon in France cannot be discussed here.) Hitler had to be defeated and the restoration and the 'economic miracle' had to occur before this function of 'left' ethics in Germany could fall into oblivion, leaving the forum of topicality open to a conformism disguised as non-conformism.

A considerable part of the leading German intelligentsia, including Adorno, have taken up residence in the 'Grand Hotel Abyss' which I described in connection with my critique of Schopenhauer as 'a beautiful hotel, equipped with every comfort, on the edge of an abyss, of nothingness, of absurdity. And the daily contemplation of the abyss between excellent meals or artistic entertainments, can only heighten the enjoyment of the subtle comforts offered.' (*Die Zerstörung der Vernunft*[8], Neuwied 1962, p. 219). The fact that Ernst Bloch continued undeterred to cling to his synthesis of 'left' ethics and 'right' epistemology (e.g. cf. *Philosophische Grundfragen I, Zur Ontologie des Noch-Nicht-Seins*[9], Frankfurt 1961) does honour to his strength of character but cannot modify the outdated nature of his theoretical position. To the extent that an authentic, fruitful and progressive opposition is really stirring in the Western world (including the Federal Republic), this opposition no longer has anything to do with the coupling of 'left' ethics with 'right' epistemology.

Thus, if anyone today reads *The Theory of the Novel* in

[8] 'The Destruction of Reason' (trans.)
[9] 'Fundamental Questions of Philosophy: The Ontology of Not-Yet-Being' (trans.)

order to become more intimately acquainted with the pre-history of the important ideologies of the 1920s and 1930s, he will derive profit from a critical reading of the book along the lines I have suggested. But if he picks up the book in the hope that it will serve him as a guide, the result will only be a still greater disorientation. As a young writer, Arnold Zweig read *The Theory of the Novel* hoping that it would help him to find his way; his healthy instinct led him, rightly, to reject it root and branch.

Georg Lukács

Budapest, July 1962.

Dedicated to Yelena Andreyevna Grabenko

I

THE FORMS OF GREAT EPIC LITERATURE EXAMINED IN RELATION TO WHETHER THE GENERAL CIVILISATION OF THE TIME IS AN INTEGRATED OR A PROBLEMATIC ONE

I

Integrated Civilisations

HAPPY ARE those ages when the starry sky is the map of all possible paths—ages whose paths are illuminated by the light of the stars. Everything in such ages is new and yet familiar, full of adventure and yet their own. The world is wide and yet it is like a home, for the fire that burns in the soul is of the same essential nature as the stars; the world and the self, the light and the fire, are sharply distinct, yet they never become permanent strangers to one another, for fire is the soul of all light and all fire clothes itself in light. Thus each action of the soul becomes meaningful and rounded in this duality: complete in meaning—in *sense*—and complete for the senses; rounded because the soul rests within itself even while it acts; rounded because its action separates itself from it and, having become itself, finds a centre of its own and draws a closed circumference round itself. 'Philosophy is really homesickness,' says Novalis: 'it is the urge to be at home everywhere.'

That is why philosophy, as a form of life or as that which determines the form and supplies the content of literary creation, is always a symptom of the rift between 'inside' and 'outside', a sign of the essential difference between the self and the world, the incongruence of soul and deed. That is why the happy ages have no philosophy, or why (it comes to the same thing) all men in such ages are philosophers, sharing the utopian aim of every philosophy. For what is the task of true philosophy if not to draw that archetypal map? What is the problem of the transcendental *locus* if not to determine how every impulse which springs from the innermost depths is co-ordinated with a form that it is ignorant of, but that has been assigned to it from eternity and that must envelop it in liberating symbols? When this is so, passion is the way, predetermined by reason, towards complete self-being and from madness come enigmatic yet decipherable messages of a transcendental power, otherwise condemned to silence. There is not yet any interiority, for there is not yet any exterior, any 'otherness' for the soul. The soul goes out to seek adventure; it lives through adventures, but it does not know the real torment of seeking and the real danger of finding; such a soul never stakes itself; it does not yet know that it can lose itself, it never thinks of having to look for itself. Such an age is the age of the epic.

It is not absence of suffering, not security of being, which in such an age encloses men and deeds in contours that are both joyful and severe (for what is meaningless and tragic in the world has not grown larger since the beginning of time; it is only that the songs of comfort ring out more loudly or are more muffled): it is the adequacy of the deeds to the soul's inner demand for greatness, for unfolding, for wholeness. When the soul does not yet know any abyss within itself which may tempt it to fall or encourage it to discover pathless heights, when the divinity that rules the world and distributes the unknown and unjust gifts of destiny is not yet understood by man, but is familiar and close to him as a father is to his small child, then every action is only a well-fitting garment for the world. Being and destiny, adventure and accomplishment, life and essence are then identical concepts. For the question which engenders the formal answers of the epic is: how can life become essence? And if no one has ever equalled Homer, nor even approached him—for, strictly speaking, his works alone are epics—it is because he found the answer before the progress of the human mind through history had allowed the question to be asked.

This line of thought can, if we wish, take us some way towards understanding the secret of the Greek world: its perfection, which is unthinkable for us, and the unbridgeable gulf that separates us from it. The Greek knew only answers but no questions, only solutions (even if enigmatic ones) but no riddles, only forms but no chaos. He drew the creative circle of forms this side of paradox, and everything which, in our time of paradox, is bound to lead to triviality, led him to perfection.

When we speak of the Greeks we always confuse the philosophy of history with aesthetics, psychology with metaphysics, and we invent a relationship between Greek forms and our own epoch. Behind those taciturn, now forever silent masks, sensitive souls look for the fugitive, elusive moments when they themselves have dreamed of peace forgetting that the value of those moments is in their very transience and that what they seek to escape from when they turn to the Greeks constitutes their own depth and greatness.

More profound minds, who try to forge an armour of purple steel out of their own streaming blood so that their wounds may be concealed forever and their heroic gesture may become a paradigm of the real heroism that is to come— so that it may call the new heroism into being—compare the fragmentariness of the forms they create with the Greeks' harmony, and their own sufferings, from which their forms have sprung, with torments which they imagine the Greeks' purity had to overcome. Interpreting formal perfection, in their obstinately solipsistic way, as a function of inner devastation, they hope to hear in the Greek words the voice of a torment whose intensity exceeds theirs by as much as Greek art is greater than their own. Yet this is a complete reversal of the transcendental topography of the mind, that topography whose nature and consequences can certainly be described, whose metaphysical significance can be interpreted and grasped, but for which it will always be impossible to find a psychology, whether of empathy or of mere understanding. For all psychological comprehension presupposes a certain position of the transcendental *loci*, and functions only within their range. Instead of trying to understand the Greek world in this way, which in the end comes to asking unconsciously: what could we do to produce these forms? or: how would we behave if we had produced these forms? it would be more fruitful to inquire into the transcendental topography of the Greek mind, which was essentially different from ours and which made those forms possible and indeed necessary.

We have said that the Greeks' answers came before their questions. This, too, should not be understood psychologically, but, at most, in terms of transcendental psychology. It means that in the ultimate structural relationship which determines all lived experience and all formal creation, there exist no qualitative differences which are insurmountable, which cannot be bridged except by a leap, between the transcendental *loci* among themselves and between them and the subject *a priori* assigned to them; that the ascent to the highest point, as also the descent to the point of utter meaninglessness, is made along the paths of adequation, that is to say, at worst, by means of a long, graduated succession of steps with many transitions from one to the next. Hence the mind's attitude within such a home is a passively visionary acceptance of ready-made, ever-present meaning. The world of meaning can be grasped, it can be taken in at a glance; all that is necessary is to find the *locus* that has been predestined for each individual. Error, here, can only be a matter of too much or too little, only a failure of measure or insight. For knowledge is only the raising of a veil, creation only the copying of visible and eternal essences, virtue a perfect knowledge of the paths; and what is alien to meaning is so only because its distance from meaning is too great.

It is a homogeneous world, and even the separation between man and world, between 'I' and 'you', cannot disturb its homogeneity. Like every other component of this rhythm, the soul stands in the midst of the world; the frontier that makes up its contours is not different in essence from the contours of things: it draws sharp, sure lines, but it separates only relatively, only in relation to and for the purpose of a homogeneous system of adequate balances. For man does not stand alone, as the sole bearer of substantiality, in the midst of reflexive forms: his relations to others and the structures which arise therefrom are as full of substance as he is himself, indeed they are more truly filled with substance because they are more general, more 'philosophic', closer and more akin to the archetypal home: love, the family, the state. What he should do or be is, for him, only a pedagogical question, an expression of the fact that he has not yet come home; it does not yet express his only, insurmountable relationship with the substance. Nor is there, within man himself, any compulsion to make the leap: he bears the stain of the distance that separates matter from substance, he will be cleansed by an immaterial soaring that will bring him closer to the substance; a long road lies before him, but within him there is no abyss.

Such frontiers necessarily enclose a rounded world. Even if menacing and incomprehensible forces become felt outside the circle which the stars of ever-present meaning draw round the cosmos to be experienced and formed, they cannot displace the presence of meaning; they can destroy life, but never tamper with being; they can cast dark shadows on the formed world, but even these are assimilated by the forms as contrasts that only bring them more clearly into relief.

The circle within which the Greeks led their metaphysical life was smaller than ours: that is why we cannot, as part of our life, place ourselves inside it. Or rather, the circle whose closed nature was the transcendental essence of their life has, for us, been broken; we cannot breathe in a closed world. We have invented the productivity of the spirit: that is why the primaeval images have irrevocably lost their objective self-evidence for us, and our thinking follows the endless path of an approximation that is never fully accomplished. We have invented the creation of forms: and that is why everything that falls from our weary and despairing hands must always be incomplete. We have found the only true substance within ourselves: that is why we have to place an unbridgeable chasm between cognition and action, between soul and created structure, between self and world, why all substantiality has to be dispersed in reflexivity on the far side of that chasm; that is why our essence had to become a postulate for ourselves and thus create a still deeper, still more menacing abyss between us and our own selves.

Our world has become infinitely large and each of its corners is richer in gifts and dangers than the world of the Greeks, but such wealth cancels out the positive meaning—the totality—upon which their life was based. For totality as the formative prime reality of every individual phenomenon implies that something closed within itself can be completed; completed because everything occurs within it, nothing is excluded from it and nothing points at a higher reality outside it; completed because everything within it ripens to its own perfection and, by attaining itself, submits to limitation. Totality of being is possible only where everything is already homogeneous before it has been contained by forms; where forms are not a constraint but only the becoming conscious, the coming to the surface of everything that had been lying dormant as a vague longing in the innermost depths of that which had to be given form; where knowledge is virtue and virtue is happiness, where beauty is the meaning of the world made visible.

That is the world of Greek philosophy. But such thinking was born only when the substance had already begun to pale. If, properly speaking, there is no such thing as a Greek aesthetic, because metaphysics anticipated everything aesthetic, then there is not, properly speaking, any difference in Greece between history and the philosophy of history: the Greeks

34

travelled in history itself through all the stages that correspond *a priori* to the great forms; their history of art is a meta-physico-genetic aesthetic, their cultural development a philosophy of history. Within this process, substance was reduced from Homer's absolute immanence of life to Plato's likewise absolute yet tangible and graspable transcendence; and the stages of the process, which are clearly and sharply distinct from one another (no gradual transitions here!) and in which the meaning of the process is laid down as though in eternal hieroglyphics—these stages are the great and timeless paradigmatic forms of world literature: epic, tragedy, philosophy. The world of the epic answers the question: how can life become essential? But the answer ripened into a question only when the substance had retreated to a far horizon. Only when tragedy had supplied the creative answer to the question: how can essence come alive? did men become aware that life as it was (the notion of life as it should be cancels out life) had lost the immanence of the essence. In form-giving destiny and in the hero who, creating himself, finds himself, pure essence awakens to life, mere life sinks into not-being in the face of the only true reality of the essence; a level of being beyond life, full of richly blossoming plentitude, has been reached, to which ordinary life cannot serve even as an antithesis. Nor was it a need or a problem which gave birth to the existence of the essence; the birth of Pallas Athene is the prototype for the emergence of Greek forms. Just as the reality of the essence, as it discharges into life and gives birth to life, betrays the loss of its pure immanence in life, so this problematic basis of tragedy becomes visible, becomes a problem, only in philosophy; only when the essence, having completely divorced itself from life, became the sole and absolute, the transcendent reality, and when the creative act of philosophy had revealed tragic destiny as the cruel and senseless arbitrariness of the empirical, the hero's passion as earth-bound and his self-accomplishment merely as the limitation of the contingent subject, did tragedy's answer to the question of life and essence appear no longer as natural and self-evident but as a miracle, a slender yet firm rainbow bridging bottomless depths.

The tragic hero takes over from Homer's living man, explaining and transfiguring him precisely because he has taken the almost extinguished torch from his hands and kindled it anew. And Plato's new man, the wise man with his active cognition and his essence-creating vision, does not merely unmask the tragic hero but also illuminates the dark peril the hero has vanquished; Plato's new wise man, by surpassing the hero, transfigures him. This new wise man, however, was the last type of man and his world was the last paradigmatic life-structure the Greek spirit was to produce. The questions which determined and supported Plato's vision became clear, yet they bore no fruit; the world became Greek in the course of time, but the Greek spirit, in that sense, has become less and less Greek; it has created new eternal problems (and solutions, too), but the essential Greek quality of τόπος νοητός is gone forever. The new spirit of destiny would indeed seem 'a folly to the Greeks'.

Truly a folly to the Greeks! Kant's starry firmament now shines only in the dark night of pure cognition, it no longer lights any solitary wanderer's path (for to be a man in the new world is to be solitary). And the inner light affords evidence of security, or its illusion, only to the wanderer's next step. No light radiates any longer from within into the world of events, into its vast complexity to which the soul is a stranger. And who can tell whether the fitness of the action to the essential nature of the subject—the only guide that still remains—really touches upon the essence, when the subject has become a phenomenon, an object unto itself; when his innermost and most particular essential nature appears to him only as a never-ceasing demand written upon the imaginary sky of that which 'should be'; when this innermost nature must emerge from an unfathomable chasm which lies within the subject himself, when only what comes up from the furthermost depths is his essential nature, and no one can ever sound or even glimpse the bottom of those depths? Art, the visionary reality of the world made to our measure, has thus become independent: it is no longer a copy, for all the models have gone; it is a created totality, for the natural unity of the metaphysical spheres has been destroyed forever.

To propose a philosophy of history relating to this transformation of the structure of the transcendental *loci* is not our intention here, nor would it be possible. This is not the place to inquire whether the reason for the change is to be found in our progress (whether upward or downward, no matter) or whether the gods of Greece were driven away by other forces. Neither do we intend to chart, however approximately, the road that led to our own reality, nor to describe the seductive power of Greece even when dead and its dazzling brilliance which, like Lucifer's, made men forget again and again the irreparable cracks in the edifice of their world and tempted them to dream of new unities—unities which contradicted the world's new essence and were therefore always doomed to come to naught. Thus the Church became a new *polis*, and the paradoxical link between the soul lost in irredeemable sin and its impossible yet certain redemption became an almost platonic ray of heavenly light in the midst of earthly reality: the leap became a ladder of earthly and heavenly hierarchies.

In Giotto and Dante, Wolfram von Eschenbach and Pisano, St. Thomas and St. Francis, the world became round once more, a totality capable of being taken in at a glance; the chasm lost the threat inherent in its actual depth; its whole darkness, without forfeiting any of its sombrely gleaming power, became pure surface and could thus be fitted easily into a closed unity of colours; the cry for redemption became a dissonance in the perfect rhythmic system of the world and thereby rendered possible a new equilibrium no less perfect than that of the Greeks: an equilibrium of mutually inadequate, heterogeneous intensities. The redeemed world, although incomprehensible and forever unattainable, was in this way brought near and given visible form. The Last Judgement became a present reality, just another element in the harmony of the spheres, which was thought to be already established; its true nature, whereby it transforms the world into a wound of Philoctetus that only the Paraclete can heal, was forgotten. A new and paradoxical Greece came into being: aesthetics became metaphysics once more.

For the first time, but also for the last. Once this unity disintegrated, there could be no more spontaneous totality of being. The source whose flood-waters had swept away the old unity was certainly exhausted; but the river beds, now dry beyond all hope, have marked forever the face of the earth.

Henceforth, any resurrection of the Greek world is a more or less conscious hypostasy of aesthetics into metaphysics— a violence done to the essence of everything that lies outside the sphere of art, and a desire to destroy it; an attempt to forget that art is only one sphere among many, and that the very disintegration and inadequacy of the world is the pre-condition for the existence of art and its becoming conscious. This exaggeration of the substantiality of art is bound to weigh too heavily upon its forms: they have to produce out of themselves all that was once simply accepted as given; in other words, before their own *a priori* effectiveness can begin to manifest itself, they must create by their own power alone the pre-conditions for such effectiveness—an object and its environment. A totality that can be simply accepted is no longer given to the forms of art: therefore they must either narrow down and volatilise whatever has to be given form to the point where they can encompass it, or else they must show polemically the impossibility of achieving their necessary object and the inner nullity of their own means. And in this case they carry the fragmentary nature of the world's structure into the world of forms.

The Problems of a Philosophy of the History of Forms

As A result of such a change in the transcendental points of orientation, art forms become subject to a historico-philosophical dialectic; the course of this dialectic will depend, however, on the *a priori* origin or 'home' of each genre. It may happen that the change affects only the object and the conditions under which it came be given form, and does not question the ultimate relationship of the form to its transcendental right to existence; when this is so, only formal changes will occur, and although they may diverge in every technical detail, they will not overturn the original form-giving principle. Sometimes, however, the change occurs precisely in the all-determining *principium stilisationis* of the genre, and then other art-forms must necessarily, for historico-philosophical reasons, correspond to the same artistic intention. This is not a matter of a change in mentality giving rise to a new genre, such as occurred in Greek history when the hero and his destiny became problematic and so brought into being the non-tragic drama of Euripides. In that case there was a complete correspondence between the subject's* *a priori* needs, his metaphysical sufferings, which provided the impulse for creation, and the pre-stabilised, eternal *locus* of the form with which the completed work coincides. The genre-creating principle which is meant here does not imply any change in mentality; rather, it forces the same mentality to turn towards a new aim which is essentially different from the old one. It means that the old parallelism of the transcendental structure

* Throughout this book, 'subject' means 'artist' or 'author', i.e., the individual whose subjectivity creates the work; 'object' means the work itself, or, sometimes, an element in the work, such as a character or plot. TRANS.

of the form-giving subject and the world of created forms has been destroyed, and the ultimate basis of artistic creation has become homeless.

German Romanticism, although it did not always completely clarify its concept of the novel, drew a close connection between it and the concept of the Romantic; and rightly so, for the novel form is, like no other, an expression of this transcendental homelessness. For the Greeks the fact that their history and the philosophy of history coincided meant that every art form was born only when the sundial of the mind showed that its hour had come, and had to disappear when the fundamental images were no longer visible on the horizon. This philosophical periodicity was lost in later times. Artistic genres now cut across one another, with a complexity that cannot be disentangled, and become traces of authentic or false searching for an aim that is no longer clearly and unequivocally given; their sum total is only a historical totality of the empirical, wherein we may seek (and possibly find) the empirical (sociological) conditions for the ways in which each form came into being, but where the historico-philosophical meaning of periodicity is never again concentrated in the forms themselves (which have become symbolic) and where this meaning can be deciphered and decoded from the totalities of various periods, but not discovered in those totalities themselves. But whereas the smallest disturbance of the transcendental correlations must cause the immanence of meaning in life to vanish beyond recovery, an essence that is divorced from life and alien to life can crown itself with its own existence in such a way that this consecration, even after a more violent upheaval, may pale but will never disappear altogether. That is why tragedy, although changed, has nevertheless survived in our time with its essential nature intact, whereas the epic had to disappear and yield its place to an entirely new form: the novel.

The complete change in our concept of life and in its relationship to essential being has, of course, changed tragedy too. It is one thing when the life-immanence of meaning vanishes with catastrophic suddenness from a pure, uncomplicated world, and quite another when this immanence is banished from the cosmos as though by the gradual working of a spell: in the latter case the longing for its return remains alive but unsatisfied; it never turns into a hopelessness rooted in certainty: therefore, the essence cannot build a tragic stage out of the felled trees of the forest of life, but must either awaken to a brief existence in the flames of a fire lit from the deadwood of a blighted life, or else must resolutely turn its back on the world's chaos and seek refuge in the abstract sphere of pure essentiality. It is the relationship of the essence to a life which, in itself, lies outside the scope of drama that renders necessary the stylistic duality of modern tragedy whose opposite poles are Shakespeare and Alfieri.

Greek tragedy stood beyond the dilemma of nearness to life as against abstraction because, for it, plenitude was not a question of coming closer to life, and transparency of dialogue did not mean the negation of its immediacy. Whatever the historical accidents or necessities that produced the Greek chorus, its artistic meaning consists in that it confers life and plenitude upon the essence situated outside and beyond all life. Thus the chorus was able to provide a background which closes the work in the same way as the marble atmospheric space between figures in a relief closes the frieze, yet the background of the chorus is also full of movement and can adapt itself to all the apparent fluctuations of a dramatic action not born of any abstract scheme, can absorb these into itself and, having enriched them with its own substance, can return them to the drama. It can make the lyrical meaning of the entire drama ring out in splendid words; it can, without suffering collapse, combine within itself the voice of lowly creature-reason, which demands tragic refutation, and the voice of the higher super-reason of destiny. Speaker and chorus in Greek tragedy are of the same fundamental essence, they are completely homogeneous with one another and can therefore fulfil completely separate functions without destroying the structure of the work; all the lyricism of the situation, of destiny, can be accumulated in the chorus, leaving to the players the all-expressive words and all-embracing gesture of the tragic dialectic laid bare—and yet they will never be separated from one another by anything other than gentle transitions. Not the remotest possibility of a certain nearness-to-life such as might destroy the dramatic form exists for either: that is why both can expand to a plenitude that has nothing schematic about it and yet is laid down *a priori*.

Life is not organically absent from modern drama; at most, it can be banished from it. But the banishment which modern classicists practise implies a recognition, not only of the existence of what is being banished, but also of its power; it is there in all the nervous words, all the gestures outbidding one another in the endeavour to keep life at bay, to remain untainted by it; invisibly and ironically, life nevertheless rules the bare, calculated severity of the structure based *a priori* on abstraction, making it narrow or confused, overexplicit or abstruse.

The other kind of tragedy consumes life. It places its heroes on the stage as living human beings in the midst of a mass of only apparently living beings, so that a clear destiny may gradually emerge incandescent from the confusion of the dramatic action, heavy with the weight of life—so that its fire may reduce to ashes everything that is merely human, so that the inexistent life of mere human beings may disintegrate into nothingness and the affective emotions of the heroic figures may flare up into a blaze of tragic passion that will anneal them into heroes free of human dross. In this way the condition of the hero has become polemical and problematic; to be a hero is no longer the natural form of existence in the sphere of essence, but the act of raising oneself above that which is merely human, whether in the surrounding mass or in the hero's own instincts. The problem of hierarchy as between life and essence, which, for Greek drama, was a formative *a priori* and therefore never became the subject of dramatic action, is thus drawn into the tragic process itself; it rends the drama into two completely heterogeneous parts which are connected with one another only by their reciprocal negation and exclusion, thus making the drama polemical and intellectual and so disturbing its very foundations. The breadth of the ground-plan thus forced upon the work and the length of the road which the hero must travel in his own soul before he discovers himself as a hero are at variance with the slenderness of construction which the dramatic form demands, and bring it closer to the epic forms; and the polemical emphasis on heroism (even in abstract tragedy) leads, of necessity, to an excess of purely lyrical lyricism.

Such lyricism has, however, yet another source which also springs from the displaced relationship between life and essence. For the Greeks, the fact that life ceased to be the home of meaning merely transferred the mutual closeness, the kinship of human beings, to another sphere, but did not destroy it: every figure in Greek drama is at the same distance from the all-sustaining essence and, therefore, is related at his deepest roots to every other figure; all understand one another because all speak the same language, all trust one another, be it as mortal enemies, for all are striving in the same way towards the same centre, and all move at the same level of an existence which is essentially the same. But when, as in modern drama, the essence can manifest and assert itself only after winning a hierarchical contest with life, when every figure carries this contest within himself as a precondition of his existence or as his motive force, then each of the *dramatis personae* can be bound to the destiny that gives him birth only by his own thread; then each must rise up from solitude and must, in irremediable solitude, hasten, in the midst of all the other lonely creatures, towards the ultimate, tragic aloneness; then, every tragic work must turn to silence without ever being understood, and no tragic deed can ever find a resonance that will adequately absorb it.

But a paradox attaches to loneliness in drama. Loneliness is the very essence of tragedy, for the soul that has attained itself through its destiny can have brothers among the stars, but never an earthly companion; yet the dramatic form of expression—the dialogue—presupposes, if it is to be many-voiced, truly dialogical, dramatic, a high degree of communion among these solitaries. The language of the absolutely lonely man is lyrical, i.e. monological; in the dialogue, the *incognito* of his soul becomes too pronounced, it overloads and swamps the clarity and definition of the words exchanged. Such loneliness is more profound than that required by the tragic form, which deals with the relationship to destiny (a relationship in which the actual, living Greek heroes had their being); loneliness has to become a problem unto itself, deepening and confusing the tragic problem and ultimately taking its place. Such loneliness is not simply the intoxication of a soul gripped by destiny and so made song; it is also the torment of a creature condemned to solitude and devoured by a longing for community.

Such loneliness gives rise to new tragic problems, especially the central problem of modern tragedy—that of trust. The new hero's soul, clothed in life yet filled with essence, can never comprehend that the essence existing within the same shell of life in another person need not be the same as his own; it knows that all those who have found one another are the same, and cannot understand that its knowledge does not come from this world, that the inner certainty of this knowledge cannot guarantee its being a constituent of this life. It has knowledge of the idea of its own self which animates it and is alive inside it, and so it must believe that the milling crowd of humanity which surrounds it is only a carnival prank and that, at the first word from the essence, the masks will fall and brothers who have hitherto been strangers to one another will fall into each other's arms. It knows this, it searches for it, and it finds only itself alone, in the midst of destiny. And so a note of reproachful, elegiac sorrow enters into its ecstasy at having found itself: a note of disappointment at a life which has not been even a caricature of what its knowledge of destiny had so clairvoyantly heralded and which gave it the strength to travel the long road alone and in darkness. This loneliness is not only dramatic but also psychological, because it is not merely the *a priori* property of all *dramatis personae* but also the lived experience of man in process of becoming a hero; and if psychology is not to remain merely raw material for drama, it can only express itself as lyricism of the soul.

Great epic writing gives form to the extensive totality of life, drama to the intensive totality of essence. That is why, when essence has lost its spontaneously rounded, sensually present totality, drama can nevertheless, in its formal *a priori* nature, find a world that is perhaps problematic but which still is all-embracing and closed within itself. But this is impossible for the great epic. For the epic, the world at any given moment is an ultimate principle; it is empirical at its deepest, most decisive, all-determining transcendental base; it can sometimes accelerate the rhythm of life, can carry something that was hidden or neglected to a utopian end which was always immanent within it, but it can never, while remaining epic, transcend the breadth and depth, the rounded, sensual, richly ordered nature of life as historically given. Any attempt at a properly utopian epic must fail because it is bound, subjectively or objectively, to transcend the empirical and spill over into the lyrical or dramatic; and such overlapping can never be fruitful for the epic.

There have been times, perhaps—certain fairly-tales still retain fragments of these lost worlds—when what today can only be reached through a utopian view was really present to the visionary eye; epic poets in those times did not have to leave the empirical in order to represent transcendent reality as the only existing one, they could be simple narrators of events, just as the Assyrians who drew winged beasts doubtless regarded themselves, and rightly, as naturalists. Already in Homer's time, however, the transcendent was inextricably interwoven with earthly existence, and Homer is inimitable precisely because, in him, this becoming-immanent was so completely successful.

This indestructible bond with reality *as it is*, the crucial difference between the epic and the drama, is a necessary consequence of the object of the epic being life itself. The concept of essence leads to transcendence simply by being posited, and then, in the transcendent, crystallises into a new and higher essence expressing through its form an essence that *should be*—an essence which, because it is born of form, remains independent of the given content of what merely *exists*. The concept of life, on the other hand, has no need of any such transcendence captured and held immobile as an object.

The worlds of essence are held high above existence by the force of forms, and their nature and contents are determined only by the inner potentialities of that force. The worlds of life stay as they are: forms only receive and mould them, only reduce them to their inborn meaning. And so these forms, which, here, can only play the role of Socrates at the birth of thoughts, can never of their own accord charm something into life that was not already present in it.

The character created by drama (this is only another way of expressing the same relationship) is the intelligible 'I' of man, the character created by the epic is the empirical 'I'.

The 'should be', in whose desperate intensity the essence seeks refuge because it has become an outlaw on earth, can objectivise itself in the intelligible 'I' as the hero's normative psychology, but in the empirical 'I' it remains a 'should be'. The power of this 'should be' is a purely psychological one, and in this it resembles the other elements of the soul; its aims are empirical, and here again it resembles other possible aspirations as given by man himself or by his environment; its contents are historical, similar to others produced in the process of time, and cannot be severed from the soil in which they have grown: they may fade, but they will never awaken to a new, ideal existence. The 'should be' kills life, and the dramatic hero assumes the symbolic attributes of the sensuous manifestations of life only in order to be able to perform the symbolic ceremony of dying in a sensuously perceptible way, making transcendence visible; yet in the epic men must be alive, or else they destroy or exhaust the very element that carries, surrounds and fills them.

(The 'should be' kills life, and every concept expresses a 'should-be' of its object; that is why thought can never arrive at a real definition of life, and why, perhaps, the philosophy of art is so much more adequate to tragedy than it is to the epic.)

The 'should be' kills life, and an epic hero constructed out of what 'should be' will always be but a shadow of the living epic man of historical reality, his shadow but never his original image, and his given world of experience and adventure can only be a watered-down copy of reality, never its core and essence. Utopian stylisation of the epic inevitably creates distance, but such distance lies between two instances of the empirical, so that the sorrow and majesty created by this distance can only make for a rhetorical tone. This distance may produce marvellous elegiac lyricism, but it can never, in itself, put real life into a content that transcends being, or turns such content into self-sufficient reality.

Whether this distance leads forward or backwards, upwards or downwards from life, it is never the creation of a new reality but always only a subjective mirroring of what already exists. Virgil's heroes lead a cool and measured shadow-existence, nourished by the blood of a splendid ardour that has sacrificed itself in order to conjure up what has vanished forever: while Zolaesque monumentality amounts only to monotonous emotion in face of the multiple yet simplified complexity of a sociological system of categories that claims to cover the whole of contemporary life.

There is such a thing as great epic literature, but drama never requires the attribute of greatness and must always resist it. The cosmos of the drama, full of its own substance, rounded with substantiality, ignores the contrast between wholeness and segment, the opposition between event and symptom: for the drama, to exist is to be a cosmos, to grasp the essence, to possess its totality. But the concept of life does not posit the necessity of the totality of life; life contains within itself both the relative independence of every separate living being from any transcendent bond and the likewise relative inevitability and indespensability of such bonds. That is why there can be epic forms whose object is not the totality of life but a segment of it, a fragment capable of independent existence. But, for the same reason, the concept of totality for the epic is not a transcendental one, as it is in drama; it is not born out of the form itself, but is empirical and metaphysical, combining transcendence and immanence inseparably within itself. In the epic, subject and object do not coincide as they do in drama, where creative subjectivity, seen from the perspective of the work, is barely a concept but only a generalised awareness; whereas in the epic subject and object are clearly and unequivocally distinct from one another and present in the work as such. And since an empirical form-giving subject follows from the empirical nature of the object seeking to acquire form, this subject can never be the basis and guarantee of the totality of the represented world. In the epic, totality can only truly manifest itself in the contents of the object: it is meta-subjective, transcendent, it is a revelation and grace. Living, empirical man is always the subject of the epic, but his creative, life-mastering arrogance is transformed in the great epics into humility, contemplation, speechless wonder at the luminous meaning which, so unexpectedly, so naturally, has become visible to him, an ordinary human being in the midst of ordinary life.

In the minor epic forms, the subject confronts the object in a more dominant and self-sufficient way. The narrator may (we cannot, nor do we intend to establish even a tentative system of epic forms here) adopt the cool and superior demeanour of the chronicler who observes the strange workings of coincidence as it plays with the destinies of men, meaningless and destructive to them, revealing and instructive to us; or he may see a small corner of the world as an ordered flower-garden in the midst of the boundless, chaotic waste-lands of life, and, moved by his vision, elevate it to the status of the sole reality; or he may be moved and impressed by the strange, profound experiences of an individual and pour them into the mould of an objectivised destiny; but whatever he does, it is his own subjectivity that singles out a fragment from the immeasurable infinity of the events of life, endows it with independent life and allows the whole from which this fragment has been taken to enter the work only as the thoughts and feelings of his hero, only as an involuntary continuation of a fragmentary causal series, only as the mirroring of a reality having its own separate existence.

Completeness in the minor epic forms is subjective: a fragment of life is transplanted by the writer into a surrounding world that emphasises it and lifts it out of the totality of life; and this selection, this delimitation, puts the stamp of its origin in the subject's will and knowledge upon the work itself: it is, more or less, lyrical in nature. The relativity of the independence and the mutual bonds of all living beings and their organic, likewise living associations can be superseded, can be elevated into form, if a conscious decision of the creative subject brings out an immanent meaning within the isolated existence of this particular fragment of life. The subject's form-giving, structuring, delimiting act, his sovereign dominance over the created object, is the lyricism of those epic forms which are without totality. Such lyricism is here the last epic unity; it is not the swallowing of a solitary 'I' in the object-free contemplation of its own self, nor is it the dissolving of the object into sensations and moods; it is born out of form, it creates form, and it sustains everything that has been given form in such a work.

The immediate, flowing power of such lyricism is bound to increase in proportion with the significance and gravity of the life-segment selected; the balance of the work is that between the positing subject and the object he singles out and elevates. In the short story, the narrative form which pin-points the strangeness and ambiguity of life, such lyricism must entirely conceal itself behind the hard outlines of the event; here, lyricism is still pure selection; the utter arbitrariness of chance, which may bring happiness or destruction but whose workings are always without reason, can only be balanced by clear, uncommented, purely objective depiction. The short story is the most purely artistic form; it expresses the ultimate meaning of all artistic creation as *mood*, as the very sense and content of the creative process, but it is rendered abstract for that very reason. It sees absurdity in all its undisguised and unadorned nakedness, and the exorcising power of this view, without fear or hope, gives it the consecration of form; meaninglessness *as meaninglessness* becomes form; it becomes eternal because it is affirmed, transcended and redeemed by form.

Between the short story and the lyric-epic forms there is a clear distinction. As soon as an event which has been given meaning by its form is, if only relatively, meaningful in its content as well, the subject, falling silent, must again struggle for words with which to build a bridge between the relative meaning of the event and the absolute. In the idyll such lyricism merges almost completely with the contours of the men and things depicted; it is this lyricism that endows these contours with the softness and airiness of a peaceful seclusion, of a blissful isolation from the storms raging in the outside world. Only when the idyll transcends its form and becomes epic, as in Goethe's and Hebbel's 'great idylls', where the whole of life with all its dangers, although modified and softened by distance, enters into the events depicted, must the author's own voice be heard and his hand must create the salutary distances, to ensure that the hard-won happiness of his heroes is not reduced to the unworthy complacency of those who cravenly turn their backs on an all-too-present wretchedness they have not overcome but only escaped, and, equally, to ensure that the dangers of life and the perturbation of its totality do not become a pale schema, reducing the triumph of deliverance to a trivial farce. And such lyricism develops into a limpid, generously flowing, all-embracing message only when the event, in its epic objectivation, becomes the vehicle and symbol of unbounded feeling; when a soul is the hero and that soul's longing is the story (once, speaking of Charles-Louis Philippe, I called such a form 'chantefable'); when the object, the event that is given form, remains isolated as indeed it should, but when the lived experience that absorbs the event and radiates it out also carries within it the ultimate meaning of life, the artist's sense-giving, life-conquering power. This power, also, is lyrical: the artist's personality, conscious and autonomous, proclaims its own interpretation of the meaning of the universe; the artist handles events as though they were instruments, he does not listen to them for a secret meaning. What is given form here is not the totality of life but the artist's relationship with that totality, his approving or condemnatory attitude towards it; here, the artist enters the arena of artistic creation as the empirical subject in all its greatness but also with all its creaturely limitations.

Neither can a totality of life which is by definition extensive be achieved by the object's being annihilated—by the subject's making itself the sole ruler of existence. However high the subject may rise above its objects and take them into its sovereign possession, they are still and always only isolated objects, whose sum never equals a real totality. Even such a subject, for all its sublime humour, remains an empirical one and its creation is only the adoption of an attitude towards its objects which, when all is said and done, remain essentially similar to itself; and the circle it draws round the world-segment thus selected and set apart defines only the limits of the subject, not of a cosmos complete in itself. The humorist's soul yearns for a more genuine substantiality than life can offer; and so he smashes all the forms and limits of life's fragile totality in order to reach the sole source of life, the pure, world-dominating 'I'. But as the objective world breaks down, so the subject, too, becomes a fragment; only the 'I' continues to exist, but its existence is then lost in the insubstantiality of its self-created world of ruins. Such subjectivity wants to give form to everything, and precisely for this reason succeeds only in mirroring a segment of the world.

This is the paradox of the subjectivity of the great epic, its 'throwing away in order to win': creative subjectivity becomes lyrical, but, exceptionally, the subjectivity which simply accepts, which humbly transforms itself into a purely receptive organ of the world, can partake of the grace of having the whole revealed to it. This is the leap that Dante made between the *Vita nuova* and the *Divina commedia*, that Goethe made between *Werther* and *Wilhelm Meister*, the leap Cervantes made when, becoming silent himself, he let the cosmic humour of *Don Quixote* become heard; by contrast, Sterne's and Jean Paul's glorious ringing voices offer no more than reflexions of a world-fragment which is merely subjective and therefore limited, narrow and arbitrary.

This is not a value judgement but an *a priori* definition of genre: the totality of life resists any attempt to find a transcendental centre within it, and refuses any of its constituent cells the right to dominate it. Only when a subject, far removed from all life and from the empirical which is necessarily posited together with life, becomes enthroned in the pure heights of essence, when it has become nothing but the carrier of the transcendental synthesis, can it contain all the conditions for totality within its own structure and transform its own limitations into the frontiers of the world. But such a subject cannot write an epic: the epic *is* life, immanence, the empirical. Dante's *Paradiso* is closer to the essence of life than Shakespeare's exuberant richness.

The synthetic power of the sphere of essence is intensified still further in the constructed totality of the dramatic problem: that which the problem decrees to be necessary, whether it be event or soul, achieves existence through its relation to the centre; the immanent dialectic of this unity accords to each individual phenomenon the essence appropriate to it depending on its distance from the centre and its relative importance to the problem. The problem here is inexpressible because it is the concrete idea of the whole, because only the polyphony of all the voices can carry the full wealth of content concealed in it. For life, the problem is an abstraction; the relationship of a character to a problem can never absorb the whole fullness of that character's life, and every event in the sphere in life can relate only allegorically to the problem. It is true that in the *Elective Affinities*, which Hebbel rightly called 'dramatic', Goethe's consummate art succeeded in weighing and ordaining everything in relation to the central problem, but even these souls, guided from the start into the problem's narrow channels, cannot attain to real existence; even this action, narrowed and cut down to fit the problem, fails to achieve a rounded totality; to fill even the fragile shell of this small world, the author is forced to introduce extraneous elements, and even if he were as successful throughout the book as he is in certain passages of supremely skilful organisation, the result would not be a totality. Likewise, the 'dramatic' concentration of Hebbel's *Song of the Nibelungs* is a splendid mistake which originated *pro domo*: a great writer's desperate effort to rescue the epic unity—disintegrating in a changed world —of an authentically epic text. Brunhilde's superhuman figure is here reduced to a mixture of woman and valkyrie, who humiliates her weak suitor, Gunther, and makes him completely questionable and feeble; only a few fairy-tale *motifs* survive the transformation of Siegfried the dragon-killer into a knightly figure. The work is saved by the problem of loyalty and revenge, that is to say by Hagen and Kriemhild. But it is a desperate, purely artistic attempt to create, with the means of composition, structuring and organisation, a unity that is no longer organically given: a desperate attempt and a heroic failure. For unity can surely be achieved, but never a real totality. In the story of the Iliad, which has no beginning and no end, a rounded universe blossoms into all-embracing life. The lucidly composed unity of the *Nibelungenlied* conceals life and decay, castles and ruins, behind its skilfully structured façade.

3

The Epic and the Novel

THE EPIC and the novel, these two major forms of great epic literature, differ from one another not by their authors' fundamental intentions but by the given historico-philosophical realities with which the authors were confronted. The novel is the epic of an age in which the extensive totality of life is no longer directly given, in which the immanence of meaning in life has become a problem, yet which still thinks in terms of totality. It would be superficial—a matter of a mere artistic technicality—to look for the only and decisive genre-defining criterion in the question of whether a work is written in verse or prose.

Verse is not an ultimate constituent either of the epic or of tragedy, although it is indeed a profound symptom by which the true nature of these forms is most truly and genuinely revealed. Tragic verse is sharp and hard, it isolates, it creates distance. It clothes the heroes in the full depth of their solitude, which is born of the form itself; it does not allow of any relationships between them except those of struggle and annihilation; its lyricism can contain notes of despair or excitement about the road yet to be travelled and its ending, it can show glimpses of the abyss over which the essential is suspended, but a purely human understanding between the tragic characters' souls will never break through, as it sometimes does in prose; the despair will never turn into elegy, nor the excitement into a longing for lost heights; the soul can never seek to plumb its own depths with psychologistic vanity, nor admire itself in the mirror of its own profundity.

Dramatic verse, as Schiller wrote to Goethe, reveals whatever triviality there may be in the artistic invention: it has a specific sharpness, a gravity all its own, in face of which nothing that is merely lifelike—which is to say nothing that is dramatically trivial—can survive: if the artist's creative mentality has anything trivial about it, the contrast between the weight of the language and that of the content will betray him.

Epic verse, too, creates distances, but in the sphere of the epic (which is the sphere of life) distance means happiness and lightness, a loosening of the bonds that tie men and objects to the ground, a lifting of the heaviness, the dullness, which are integral to life and which are dispersed only in scattered happy moments. The created distances of epic verse transform such moments into the true level of life. And so the effect of verse is here the opposite just because its immediate consequences—that of abolishing triviality and coming closer to the essence—is the same. Heaviness is trivial in the sphere of life—the epic—just as lightness is trivial in tragedy. An objective guarantee that the complete removal of everything life-like does not mean an empty abstraction from life but the becoming essence, can only be given the consistency with which these unlifelike forms are created; only if they are incomparably more fulfilled, more rounded, more fraught with substance than we could ever dream of in real life, can it be said that tragic stylisation has been successfully achieved. Everything light or pallid (which of course has nothing to do with the banal concept of unlifelikeness) reveals the absence of a normative tragic intention and so demonstrates the triviality of the work, whatever the psychological subtlety and/or lyrical delicacy of its parts.

In life, however, heaviness means the absence of present meaning, a hopeless entanglement in senseless casual connections, a withered sterile existence too close to the earth and too far from heaven, a plodding on, an inability to liberate oneself from the bonds of sheer brutal materiality, everything that, for the finest immanent forces of life, represents a challenge which must be constantly overcome—it is, in terms of formal value judgement, triviality. A pre-stabilised harmony decrees that epic verse should sing of the blessedly existent totality of life; the pre-poetic process of embracing all life in a mythology had liberated existence from all trivial heaviness; in Homer, the spring buds were only just opening, ready to blossom. Verse itself, however, can only tentatively encourage the bud to open; verse can only weave a garland of freedom round something that has already been liberated from all fetters. If the author's action consists in disclosing buried meaning, if his heroes must first break out of their prisons and, in desperate struggles or long, wearisome wanderings, attain the home of their dreams—their freedom from terrestrial gravity—then the power of verse, which can spread a carpet of flowers over the chasm, is not sufficient to build a practicable road across it. The lightness of great epic literature is only the concretely immanent utopia of the historical hour, and the form-giving detachment which verse as a vehicle confers upon whatever it carries must, therefore, rob the epic of its great totality, its subjectlessness, and transform it into an idyll or a piece of playful lyricism. The lightness of great epic literature is a positive value and a reality-creating force only if the restraining bonds have really been thrown off. Great epic literature is never the result of men forgetting their enslavement in the lovely play of a liberated imagination or in tranquil retirement to happy isles not to be found on the map of this world of trivial attachment. In times to which such lightness is no longer given, verse is banished from the great epic, or else it transforms itself, unexpectedly and unintentionally, into lyric verse. Only prose can then encompass the suffering and the laurels, the struggle and the crown, with equal power; only its unfettered plasticity and

its non-rhythmic rigour can, with equal power, embrace the
fetters and the freedom, the given heaviness and the conquered lightness of a world henceforth immanently radiant
with found meaning. It is no accident that the disintegration
of a reality-become-song led, in Cervantes' prose, to the
sorrowful lightness of a great epic, whereas the serene dance
of Ariosto's verse remained mere lyrical play; it is no accident that Goethe, the epic poet, poured his idylls into the
mould of verse but chose prose for the totality of his
Meister (master) novel. In the world of distances, all epic
verse turns into lyric poetry (*Don Juan* and *Onegin*, although written in verse, belong to the company of the
great humorous novels), for, in verse, everything hidden
becomes manifest, and the swift flight of verse makes the
distance over which prose travels with its deliberate pace
as it gradually approaches meaning appear naked, mocked,
trampled, or merely a forgotten dream.

Dante's verse, too, is not lyrical although it is more lyrical
than Homer's; it intensifies and concentrates the ballad
tone into an epic one. The immanence of the meaning of
life is present and existent in Dante's world, but only
in the beyond: it is the perfect immanence of the transcendent.

Distance in the ordinary world of life is extended to the
point where it cannot be overcome, but beyond that world
every lost wanderer finds the home that has awaited him
since all eternity; every solitary voice that falls silent on
earth is there awaited by a chorus that takes it up, carries
it towards harmony and, through it, becomes harmony
itself.

The world of distances lies sprawling and chaotic beneath
the radiant celestial rose of sense made sensuous; it is visible
and undisguised at every moment. Every inhabitant of that
home in the beyond has come from this world, each is
bound to it by the indissoluble force of destiny, but each

recognises it, sees it in its fragility and heaviness, only when he has travelled to the end of his path thereby made meaning-ful; every figure sings of its isolated destiny, the isolated event in which its apportioned lot was made manifest: a ballad. And just as the totality of the transcendent world-structure is the pre-determined sense-giving, all-embracing *a priori* of each individual destiny, so the increasing com-prehension of this edifice, its structure and its beauty—the great experience of Dante the traveller—envelops every-thing in the unity of its meaning, now revealed. Dante's insight transforms the individual into a component of the whole, and so the ballads become epic songs. The meaning of this world becomes distanceless, visible and immanent only in the beyond. Totality, in this world, is bound to be a fragile or merely a longed-for one: the verse passages in Wolfram von Eschenbach or Gottfried von Strassburg are only lyrical ornaments to their novels, and the ballad quality of the *Song of the Nibelungs* can be disguised by compo-sitional means, but cannot be rounded so that it achieves world-embracing totality.

The epic gives form to a totality of life that is rounded from within; the novel seeks, by giving form, to uncover and construct the concealed totality of life. The given structure of the object (i.e. the search, which is only a way of expressing the subject's recognition that neither objective life nor its relationship to the subject is spontaneously har-monious in itself) supplies an indication of the form-giving intention. All the fissures and rents which are inherent in the historical situation must be drawn into the form-giving process and cannot nor should be disguised by compo-sitional means. Thus the fundamental form-determining in-tention of the novel is objectivised as the psychology of the novel's heroes: they are seekers. The simple fact of seeking implies that neither the goals nor the way leading to them can be directly given, or else that, if they are given in a psychologically direct and solid manner, this is not evidence of really existent relations or ethical necessities but only of a psychological fact to which nothing in the world of objects or norms need necessarily correspond. To put it another way, this 'givenness' may be crime or madness; the boundaries which separate crime from acclaimed heroism and madness from life-mastering wisdom are tentative, purely psychological ones, although at the end, when the aberration makes itself terribly manifest and clear, there is no longer any confusion.

In this sense, the epic and the tragedy know neither crime nor madness. What the customary concepts of everyday life call crime is, for them, either not there at all, or it is nothing other than the point, symbolically fixed and sensually perceptible from afar, at which the soul's relationship to its destiny, the vehicle of its metaphysical homesickness, becomes visible. The epic world is either a purely childlike one in which the transgression of stable, traditional norms has to entail vengeance which again must be avenged *ad infinitum*, or else it is the perfect theodicy in which crime and punishment lie in the scales of world justice as equal, mutually homogeneous weights.

In tragedy crime is either nothing at all or a symbol— it is either a mere element of the action, demanded and determined by technical laws, or it is the breaking down of forms on this side of the essence, it is the entrance through which the soul comes into its own. Of madness the epic knows nothing, unless it be the generally incomprehensible language of a superworld that possesses no other means of expression. In non-problematic tragedy, madness can be the symbolic expression of an end, equivalent to physical death or to the living death of a soul consumed by the essential fire of selfhood. For crime and madness are objectivations of transcendental homelessness—the homelessness of an action in the human order of social relations, the homelessness of a soul in the ideal order of a supra-personal system of values. Every form is the resolution of a fundamental dissonance of existence; every form restores the absurd to its proper place as the vehicle, the necessary condition of meaning. When the peak of absurdity, the futility of genuine and profound human aspirations, or the possibility of the ultimate nothingness of man has to be absorbed into literary form as a basic vehicular fact, and when what is in itself absurd has to be explained and analysed and, consequently, recognised as being irreducibly *there*, then, although some streams within such a form may flow into a sea of fulfilment, the absence of any manifest aim, the determining lack of direction of life as a whole, must be the basic *a priori* constituent, the fundamental structural element of the characters and events within it.

Where no aims are directly given, the structures which the soul, in the process of *becoming-man*, encounters as the arena and sub-stratum of its activity among men lose their obvious roots in supra-personal ideal necessities; they are simply existent, perhaps powerful, perhaps frail, but they neither carry the consecration of the absolute within them nor are they the natural containers for the overflowing interiority of the soul. They form the world of convention, a world from whose all-embracing power only the innermost recesses of the soul are exempt, a world which is present everywhere in a multiplicity of forms too complex for understanding. Its strict laws, both in becoming and in being, are necessarily evident to the cognisant subject, but despite its regularity, it is a world that does not offer itself either as meaning to the aim-seeking subject or as matter, in sensuous immediacy, to the active subject. It is a second nature, and, like nature (first nature), it is determinable only as the embodiment of recognised but senseless necessities and therefore it is incomprehensible, unknowable in its real substance. Yet for creative literature substance alone has existence and only substances

which are profoundly homogeneous with one another can
enter into the fighting union of reciprocal compositional relationships.

Lyric poetry can ignore the phenomenalisation of the
first nature and can create a protean mythology of substantial
subjectivity out of the constitutive strength of its ignorance.
In lyric poetry, only the great moment exists, the moment at
which the meaningful unity of nature and soul or their
meaningful divorce, the necessary and affirmed loneliness of
the soul becomes eternal. At the lyrical moment the purest
interiority of the soul, set apart from duration without choice,
lifted above the obscurely-determined multiplicity of things,
solidifies into substance; whilst alien, unknowable nature is
driven from within, to agglomerate into a symbol that is
illuminated throughout. Yet this relationship between soul
and nature can be produced only at lyrical moments. Otherwise, nature is transformed—because of its lack of meaning
—into a kind of picturesque lumber-room of sensuous symbols
for literature; it seems to be fixed in its bewitched mobility
and can only be reduced to a meaningfully animated calm by
the magic word of lyricism. Such moments are constitutive
and form-determining only for lyric poetry; only in lyric
poetry do these direct, sudden flashes of the substance become
like lost original manuscripts suddenly made legible; only in
lyric poetry is the subject, the vehicle of such experiences,
transformed into the sole carrier of meaning, the only true
reality. Drama is played out in a sphere that lies beyond such
reality, and in the epic forms the subjective experience remains inside the subject: it becomes mood. And nature, bereft
of its 'senseless' autonomous life as well of its meaningful
symbolism, becomes a background, a piece of scenery, an
accompanying voice; it has lost its independence and is
only a sensually perceptible projection of the essential—of
interiority.

The second nature, the nature of man-made structures, has

no lyrical substantiality; its forms are too rigid to adapt themselves to the symbol-creating moment; the content of the second nature, precipitated by its own laws, is too definite to be able to rid itself of those elements which, in lyric poetry, are bound to become essayistic; furthermore, these elements are so much at the mercy of laws, are so absolutely devoid of any sensuous valency of existence independent from laws, that without them they can only disintegrate into nothingness. This second nature is not dumb, sensuous and yet senseless like the first: it is a complex of senses—meanings —which has become rigid and strange, and which no longer awakens interiority; it is a charnel-house of long-dead interiorities; this second nature could only be brought to life— if this were possible—by the metaphysical act of reawakening the souls which, in an early or ideal existence, created or preserved it; it can never be animated by another interiority. It is too akin to the soul's aspirations to be treated by the soul as mere raw material for moods, yet too alien to those aspirations ever to become their appropriate and adequate expression. Estrangement from nature (the first nature), the modern sentimental attitude to nature, is only a projection of man's experience of his self-made environment as a prison instead of as a parental home.

When the structures made by man for man are really adequate to man, they are his necessary and native home; and he does not know the nostalgia that posits and experiences nature as the object of its own seeking and finding. The first nature, nature as a set of laws for pure cognition, nature as the bringer of comfort to pure feeling, is nothing other than the historico-philosophical objectivation of man's alienation from his own constructs.

When the soul-content of these constructs can no longer directly become soul, when the constructs no longer appear as the agglomerate and concentrate of interiorities which can at any moment be transformed back into a soul, then they must, in order to subsist, achieve a power which dominates men blindly, without exception or choice. And so men call 'law' the recognition of the power that holds them in thrall, and they conceptualise as 'law' their despair at its omnipotence and universality: conceptualise it into a sublime and exalting logic, a necessity that is eternal, immutable and beyond the reach of man.

The nature of laws and the nature of moods stem from the same *locus* in the soul: they presuppose the impossibility of an attained and meaningful substance, the impossibility of finding a constitutive object adequate to the constitutive subject. In its experience of nature, the subject, which alone is real, dissolves the whole outside world in mood, and itself becomes mood by virtue of the inexorable identity of essence between the contemplative subject and its object. The desire to know a world cleansed of all wanting and all willing transforms the subject into an a-subjective, constructive and constructing embodiment of cognitive functions. This is bound to be so, for the subject is constitutive only when it acts from within—i.e. only the ethical subject is constitutive. It can only avoid falling prey to laws and moods if the arena of its actions, the normative object of its actions, is made of the stuff of pure ethics: if right and custom are identical with morality: if no more of the soul has to be put into the man-made structures to make them serve as man's proper sphere of action than can be released, by action, from those structures. Under such conditions the soul has no need to recognise any laws, for the soul itself is the law of man and man will behold the same face of the same soul upon every substance against which he may have to prove himself. Under such conditions, it would seem petty and futile to try to overcome the strangeness of the non-human world by the mood-arousing power of the subject: the world of man that matters is the one where the soul, as man, god or demon, is at home: then the soul finds everything it needs, it does not have to create or animate anything out of its own self, for its existence is filled to overbrimming with the finding, gathering and moulding of all that is given as cognate to the soul.

The epic individual, the hero of the novel, is the product of estrangement from the outside world. When the world is internally homogeneous, men do not differ qualitatively from one another; there are of course heroes and villains, pious men and criminals, but even the greatest hero is only a head taller than the mass of his fellows, and the wise man's dignified words are heard even by the most foolish. The autonomous life of interiority is possible and necessary only when the distinctions between men have made an unbridgeable chasm; when the gods are silent and neither sacrifices nor the ecstatic gift of tongues can solve their riddle; when the world of deeds separates itself from men and, because of this independence, becomes hollow and incapable of absorbing the true meaning of deeds in itself, incapable of becoming a symbol through deeds and dissolving them in turn into symbols; when interiority and adventure are forever divorced from one another.

The epic hero is, strictly speaking, never an individual. It is traditionally thought that one of the essential characteristics of the epic is the fact that its theme is not a personal destiny but the destiny of a community. And rightly so, for the completeness, the roundness of the value system which determines the epic cosmos creates a whole which is too organic for any part of it to become so enclosed within itself, so dependent upon itself, as to find itself as an interiority— i.e. to become a personality. The omnipotence of ethics, which posits every soul as autonomous and incomparable, is still unknown in such a world. When life *quae* life finds an immanent meaning in itself, the categories of the organic determine everything: an individual structure and physiognomy is simply the product of a balance between the part and the whole, mutually determining one another; it is never the product of polemical self-contemplation by the lost and lonely personality. The significance which an event can have in a world that is rounded in this way is therefore always a quantitative one; the series of adventures in which the event expresses itself has weight in so far as it is significant to a great organic life complex—a nation or a family.

Epic heroes have to be kings for different reasons from the heroes of tragedy (although these reasons are also formal). In tragedy the hero must be a king simply because of the need to sweep all the petty causalities of life from the onto-logical path of destiny—because the socially dominant figure is the only one whose conflicts, while retaining the sensuous illusion of a symbolic existence, grow solely out of the tragic problem; because only such a figure can be surrounded, even as to the forms of its external appearance, with the required atmosphere of significant isolation.

What is a symbol in tragedy becomes a reality in the epic: the weight of the bonds linking an individual destiny to a totality. World destiny, which in tragedy is merely the number of noughts that have to be added to 1 to transform it into a million, is what actually gives the events of the epic their content; the epic hero, as bearer of his destiny, is not lonely, for this destiny connects him by indissoluble threads to the community whose fate is crystallised in his own.

As for the community, it is an organic—and therefore intrinsically meaningful—concrete totality; that is why the substance of adventure in an epic is always articulated, never strictly closed; this substance is an organism of infinite interior richness, and in this is identical or similar to the substance of other adventure.

The way Homer's epics begin in the middle and do not finish at the end is a reflexion of the truly epic mentality's total indifference to any form of architectural construction, and the introduction of extraneous themes—such as that of

Dietrich von Born in the Song of the Nibelungs—can never disturb this balance, for everything in the epic has a life of its own and derives its completeness from its own inner significance. The extraneous can calmly hold out its hand to the central; mere contact between concrete things creates concrete relationships, and the extraneous, because of its perspectival distance and its not yet realised richness, does not endanger the unity of the whole and yet has obvious organic existence.

Dante is the only great example in which we see the architectural clearly conquering the organic, and therefore he represents a historico-philosophical transition from the pure epic to the novel. In Dante there is still the perfect immanent distancelessness and completeness of the true epic, but his figures are already individuals, consciously and energetically placing themselves in opposition to a reality that is becoming closed to them, individuals who, through this opposition, become real personalities. The constituent principle of Dante's totality is a highly systematic one, abolishing the epic independence of the organic part-unities and transforming them into hierarchically ordered, autonomous parts. Such individuality, it is true, is found more in the secondary figures than in the hero. The tendency of each part-unity to retain its autonomous lyrical life (a category unknown and unknowable in the old epic) increases towards the periphery as the distance from the centre becomes greater.

The combination of the presuppositions of the epic and the novel and their synthesis to an *epopoeia* is based on the dual structure of Dante's world: the break between life and meaning is surpassed and cancelled by the coincidence of life and meaning in a present, actually experienced transcendence. To the postulate-free organic nature of the older epics, Dante opposes a hierarchy of fulfilled postulates. Dante—and only Dante—did not have to endow his hero with visible social superiority or with a heroic destiny that co-determined the destiny of the community—because his hero's lived experience was the symbolic unity of human destiny in general.

4

The Inner Form of the Novel

THE TOTALITY of Dante's world is the totality of a visual system of concepts. It is because of this sensual 'thingness', this substantiality both of the concepts themselves and of their hierarchical order within the system, that completeness and totality can become constitutive structural categories rather than regulative ones: because of it, the progression through the totality is a voyage which, although full of suspense, is a well-conducted and safe one; and, because of it, it was possible for an epic to be created at a time when the historico-philosophical situation was already beginning to demand the novel. In a novel, totality can be systematised only in abstract terms, which is why any system that could be established in the novel—a system being, after the final disappearance of the organic, the only possible form of a rounded totality—had to be one of abstract concepts and therefore not directly suitable for aesthetic form-giving. Such abstract systematisation is, it is true, the ultimate basis of the entire structure, but in the created reality of the novel all that becomes visible is the distance separating the systematisation from concrete life: a systematisation which emphasises the conventionality of the objective world and the interiority of the subjective one. Thus the elements of the novel are, in the Hegelian sense, entirely abstract; abstract, the nostalgia of the characters for utopian perfection, a nostalgia that feels itself and its desires to be the only true reality; abstract, the existence of social structures based only upon their factual presence and their sheer ability to continue; abstract, finally, the form-giving intention which, instead of surmounting the distance between these two abstract groups of elements, allows it to subsist, which does not even attempt to surmount it but renders it sensuous as the lived experience of the novel's characters, uses it as a means of connecting the two groups and so turns it into an instrument of composition.

We have already recognised the dangers that arise from the fundamentally abstract nature of the novel: the risk of overlapping into lyricism or drama, the risk of narrowing reality so that the work becomes an idyll, the risk of sinking to the level of mere entertainment literature. These dangers can be resisted only by positing the fragile and incomplete nature of the world as ultimate reality: by recognising, consciously and consistently, everything that points outside and beyond the confines of the world.

Every art form is defined by the metaphysical dissonance of life which it accepts and organises as the basis of a totality complete in itself; the mood of the resulting world, and the atmosphere in which the persons and events thus created have their being, are determined by the danger which arises from this incompletely resolved dissonance and which therefore threatens the form. The dissonance special to the novel, the refusal of the immanence of being to enter into empirical life, produces a problem of form whose formal nature is much less obvious than in other kinds of art, and which, because it looks like a problem of content, needs to be approached by both ethical and aesthetic arguments, even more than do problems which are obviously purely formal.

The novel is the art-form of virile maturity, in contrast to the normative childlikeness of the epic (the drama form, being in the margin of life, is outside the ages of man even if these are conceived as *a priori* categories or normative stages). The novel is the art-form of virile maturity: this means that the completeness of the novel's world, if seen objectively, is an imperfection, and if subjectively experienced, it amounts to resignation. The danger by which the novel is determined is twofold: either the fragility of the world may manifest itself so crudely that it will cancel out the immanence of meaning which the form demands, or else the longing for the dissonance to be resolved, affirmed and absorbed into the work may be so great that it will lead to a premature closing of the circle of the novel's world, causing the form to disintegrate into disparate, heterogeneous parts. The fragility of the world may be superficially disguised but it cannot be abolished; consequently this fragility will appear in the novel as unprocessed raw material, whose weak cohesion will have been destroyed. In either case the structure remains abstract: the abstract basis of the novel assumes form as a result of the abstraction seeing through itself; the immanence of meaning required by the form is attained precisely when the author goes all the way, ruthlessly, towards exposing its absence.

Art always says 'And yet!' to life. The creation of forms is the most profound confirmation of the existence of a dissonance. But in all other genres—even, for reasons we can now understand, in the epic—this affirmation of a dissonance precedes the act of form-giving, whereas in the novel it is the form itself. That is why the relationship between ethics and aesthetics in the creative process of the novel is different from what it is in other kinds of literature. There, ethic is a purely formal pre-condition which, by its depth, allows the form-determined essence to be attained and, by its breadth, renders possible a totality which is likewise determined by the form and which, by its all-embracing nature, establishes a balance between the constituent elements—a balance for which 'justice' is only a term in the language of pure ethics. In the novel, on the other hand, ethic—the ethical intention—is visible in the creation of every detail and hence is, in its most concrete content, an effective structural element of the work itself.

Thus, the novel, in contrast to others genres whose existence resides within the finished form, appears as something in process of becoming. That is why, from the artistic view-point, the novel is the most hazardous genre, and why it has been described as only half an art by many who equate *having a problematic* with *being problematic*. The description may seem convincing because the novel—unlike other genres —has a caricatural twin almost indistinguishable from itself in all inessential formal characteristics: the entertainment novel, which has all the outward features of the novel but which, in essence, is bound to nothing and based on nothing, i.e. is entirely meaningless. Other genres, where being is treated as already attained, cannot have such a caricatural twin because the extra-artistic element of its creation can never be disguised even for a moment; whereas with the novel, because of the regulative, hidden nature of the effective binding and forming ideas, because of the apparent resemblance of empty animation to a process whose ultimate content cannot be rationalised, superficial likeness can almost lead to the caricature being mistaken for the real thing. But a closer look will always, in any concrete case, reveal the caricature for what it is.

Other arguments used to deny the genuinely artistic nature of the novel likewise enjoy only a semblance of truth—not only because the normative incompleteness, the problematic nature of the novel is a true-born form in the historico-philosophical sense and proves its legitimacy by attaining its substratum, the true condition of the contemporary spirit, but also because its nature as a process excludes complete-ness only so far as content is concerned. As form, the novel establishes a fluctuating yet firm balance between becoming and being; as the idea of becoming, it becomes a state. Thus the novel, by transforming itself into a normative being of becoming, surmounts itself. 'The voyage is completed: the way begins.'

The 'half-art' of the novel, therefore, prescribes still stricter, still more inviolable artistic laws for itself than do the power in the world if men did not sometimes fall prey to the more indefinable and unformulable they are in their very essence: they are laws of tact. Tact and taste, in themselves subordinate categories which belong wholly to the sphere of mere life and are irrelevant to an essential ethical world, here acquire great constitutive significance: only through them is subjectivity, at the beginning of the novel's totality and at its end, capable of maintaining itself in equilibrium, of positing itself as epically normative objectivity and thus of surmounting abstraction, the inherent danger of the novel form.

This danger can also be formulated in another way: where ethic has to carry the structure of a form as a matter of content and not merely as a formal *a priori*, and where a coincidence, or at least a marked convergence between ethic as an interior factor of life and its substratum of action in the social structures, is not given as it was in the epic ages, there is a danger that, instead of an existent totality, only a subjective aspect of that totality will be given form, obscuring or even destroying the creative intention of acceptance and objectivity which the great epic demands. This danger cannot be circumvented but can only be overcome from within. For such subjectivity is not eliminated if it remains unexpressed or is transformed into a will for objectivity: such a silence, such a will, is even more subjective than the overt manifestation of a clearly conscious subjectivity, and therefore, in the Hegelian sense, even more abstract.

The self-recognition and, with it, self-abolition of subjectivity was called irony by the first theoreticians of the novel, the aesthetic philosophers of early Romanticism. As a formal constituent of the novel form this signifies an interior diversion of the normatively creative subject into a subjectivity as interiority, which opposes power complexes that are alien to it and which strives to imprint the contents of its longing upon the alien world, and a subjectivity which sees through the abstract and, therefore, limited nature of the

74

mutually alien worlds of subject and object, understand these worlds by seeing their limitations as necessary conditions of their existence and, by thus seeing through them, allows the duality of the world to subsist. At the same time the creative subjectivity glimpses a unified world in the mutual relativity of elements essentially alien to one another, and gives form to this world. Yet this glimpsed unified world is nevertheless purely formal; the antagonistic nature of the inner and outer worlds is not abolished but only recognised as necessary; the subject which recognises it as such is just as empirical— just as much part of the outside world, confined in its own interiority—as the characters which have become its objects. Such irony is free from that cold and abstract superiority which narrows down the objective form to a subjective one and reduces the totality to a mere aspect of itself; this is the case in satire. In the novel the subject, as observer and creator, is compelled by irony to apply its recognition of the world to itself and to treat itself, like its own creatures, as a free object of free irony: it must transform itself into a purely receptive subject, as is normatively required for great epic literature.

The irony of the novel is the self-correction of the world's fragility: inadequate relations can transform themselves into a fanciful yet well-ordered round of misunderstandings and cross-purposes, within which everything is seen as many-sided, within which things appear as isolated and yet connected, as full of value and yet totally devoid of it, as abstract fragments and as concrete autonomous life, as flowering and as decaying, as the infliction of suffering and as suffering itself.

Thus a new perspective of life is reached on an entirely new basis—that of the indissoluble connection between the relative independence of the parts and their attachment to the whole. But the parts, despite this attachment, can never lose their inexorable, abstract self-dependence: and their

75

relationship to the totality, although it approximates as closely as possible to an organic one, is nevertheless not a true-born organic relationship but a conceptual one which is abolished again and again.

The consequence of this, from the compositional point of view, is that, although the characters and their actions possess the infinity of authentic epic literature, their structure is essentially different from that of the epic. The structural difference in which this fundamentally conceptual pseudo-organic nature of the material of the novel finds expression is the difference between something that is homogeneously organic and stable and something that is heterogeneously contingent and discrete. Because of this contingent nature, the relatively independent parts are more independent, more self-contained than those of the epic and must therefore, if they are not to destroy the whole, be inserted into it by means which transcend their mere presence. In contrast to the epic, they must have a strict compositional and architectural significance, whether this takes the form of contrasting lights thrown upon the central problem (as with the *novellas* included in *Don Quixote*) or of the introduction, by way of a prelude, of hidden motifs which are to be decisive at the end (as with the *Confessions of a Beautiful Soul*). The existence of the relatively independent parts can never be justified by their mere presence.

The ability of parts which are only compositionally united to have discrete autonomous life is, of course, significant only as a symptom, in that it renders the structure of the novel's totality clearly visible. It is by no means necessary in itself for every exemplary novel to exhibit this extreme consequence of the novel's structure. Any attempt to surmount the problematic of the novel by insisting exclusively on this specific aspect must, in fact, lead to artificiality and to excessive obviousness of composition, as with the Romantics or with the first novel of Paul Ernst.

This aspect is only a symptom of contingency; it merely sheds light upon a state of affairs which is necessarily present at all times and everywhere, but which is covered over, by skilfully ironic compositional tact, by a semblance of organic quality which is revealed again and again as illusory.

The outward form of the novel is essentially biographical. The fluctuation between a conceptual system which can never completely capture life and a life complex which can never attain completeness because completeness is immanently utopian, can be objectivised only in that organic quality which is the aim of biography. In a world situation where the organic was the all-dominating category of existence, to make the individuality of a living being, with all its limitations, the starting point of stylisation and the centre of form-giving would have seemed foolish—a gratuitous violence inflicted upon the organic. In an age of constitutive systems, the exemplary significance of an individual life could never be anything more than an example: to represent it as the vehicle of values rather than as their substratum, assuming even that such a project might have been conceived, would have been an act of the most ridiculous arrogance. In the biographical form, the separate being—the individual—has a specific weight which would have been too high for the predominance of life, too low for the absolute predominance of the system; his degree of isolation would have been too great for the former, meaningless for the latter; his relationship to the ideal of which he is the carrier and the agent would have been over-emphatic for the former, insufficiently subordinated for the latter.

In the biographical form, the unfulfillable, sentimental striving both for the immediate unity of life and for a completely rounded architecture of the system is balanced and brought to rest: it is transformed into being. The central character of a biography is significant only by his relationship to a world of ideals that stands above him: but this world, in turn, is realised only through its existence within that individual and his lived experience. Thus in the biographical form the balance of both spheres which are unrealised and unrealisable in isolation produces a new and autonomous life that is, however paradoxically, complete in itself and immanently meaningful: the life of the problematic individual.

The contingent world and the problematic individual are realities which mutually determine one another. If the individual is unproblematic, then his aims are given to him with immediate obviousness, and the realisation of the world constructed by these given aims may involve hindrances and difficulties but never any serious threat to his interior life. Such a threat arises only when the outside world is no longer adapted to the individual's ideas and the ideas become subjective facts—*ideals*—in his soul. The positing of ideas as unrealisable and, in the empirical sense, as unreal, i.e. their transformation into ideals, destroys the immediate problem-free organic nature of the individual. Individuality then becomes an aim unto itself because it finds within itself everything that is essential to it and that make its life autonomous —even if what it finds can never be a firm possession or the basis of its life, but is an object of search. The surrounding world of the individual, however, is the substratum and material of the same categorical forms upon which his interior world is based, and differs from them only in its content; therefore the unbridgeable chasm between the reality that is and the ideal that should be must represent the essence of the outside world, the difference of their materials being only a structural one. This difference manifests itself most clearly in the pure negativity of the ideal. In the subjective world of the soul the ideal is as much at home as the soul's other realities, But, at the level of the soul, the ideal by entering lived experience can play, even in its content, a directly positive role; whereas in the outside world the gap between reality and the ideal becomes apparent only by the absence of the ideal, in the immanent self-criticism of mere reality caused by that absence; in the self-revelation of the nothingness of mere reality without an immanent ideal.

This self-destruction of reality, which, as given, is of an entirely intellectual dialectical nature and is not immediately evident in a poetic and sensuous way, appears in two different forms. First, as disharmony between the interiority of the individual and the substratum of his actions; the more genuine is the interiority and the nearer its sources are to the ideas of life which, in the soul, have turned into ideals, the more clearly this disharmony will appear. Second, as the inability of the outside world, which is a stranger to ideals and an enemy of interiority, to achieve real completeness; an inability to find either the form of totality for itself as a whole, or any form of coherence for its own relationship to its elements and their relationship to one another: in other words, the outside world cannot be represented. Both the parts and the whole of such an outside world defy any forms of directly sensuous representation. They acquire life only when they can be related either to the life-experiencing interiority of the individual lost in their labyrinth, or to the observing and creative eye of the artist's subjectivity: when they become objects of mood or reflexion.

This is the formal reason and the literary justification for the Romantics' demand that the novel, combining all genres within itself, should include pure lyric poetry and pure thought in its structure. The discrete nature of the outside world demands, for the sake of epic significance and sensuous valency, the inclusion of elements some of which are essentially alien to epic literature while others are alien to imaginative literature in general. The inclusion of these elements is not merely a question of lyrical atmosphere and intellectual significance being added to otherwise prosaic, isolated and inessential events. Only in these elements can the ultimate basis of the whole, the basis which holds the entire work together, become visible: the system of regulative ideas which constitutes the totality. For the discrete structure of the outside world is due, in the last analysis, to the fact that any system of ideas has only regulative power vis-à-vis reality. The incapacity of ideas to penetrate reality makes reality heterogeneous and discrete. And this incapacity creates a still more profound need for the elements of reality to have some definite relationship to a system of ideas than was the case in Dante's world. There, life and meaning were conferred upon each event by allocating to each its place in the world's architecture, just as directly as, in Homer's organic world, life and meaning were present with perfect immanence in every manifestation of life.

The inner form of the novel has been understood as the process of the problematic individual's journeying towards himself, the road from dull captivity within a merely present reality—a reality that is heterogeneous in itself and meaningless to the individual—towards clear self-recognition. After such self-recognition has been attained, the ideal thus formed irradiates the individual's life as its immanent meaning; but the conflict between what is and what should be has not been abolished and cannot be abolished in the sphere wherein these events take place—the life sphere of the novel; only a maximum conciliation—the profound and intensive irradiation of a man by his life's meaning—is attainable. The immanence of meaning which the form of the novel requires lies in the hero's finding out through experience that a mere glimpse of meaning is the highest that life has to offer, and that this glimpse is the only thing worth the commitment of an entire life, the only thing by which the struggle will have been justified. The process of finding out extends over a lifetime, and its direction and scope are given with its normative content, the way towards a man's recognition of himself. The inner shape of the process and the most adequate means of shaping it—the biographical form—reveal the great difference between the discrete, unlimited nature of the material of the novel and the continuum-like infinity of the material of the epic. This lack of limits in the novel has a 'bad' infinity about it: therefore it needs certain imposed limits in order to become form; whereas the infinity of purely epic matter is an inner, organic one, it is itself a carrier of value, it puts emphasis on value, it sets its own limits for itself and from within itself, and the outward infinity of its range is almost immaterial to it—only a consequence and, at most, a symptom.

The novel overcomes its 'bad' infinity by recourse to the biographical form. On the one hand, the scope of the world is limited by the scope of the hero's possible experiences and its mass is organised by the orientation of his development towards finding the meaning of life in self-recognition; on the other hand, the discretely heterogeneous mass of isolated persons, non-sensuous structures and meaningless events receives a unified articulation by the relating of each separate element to the central character and the problem symbolised by the story of his life.

The beginning and the end of the world of a novel, which are determined by the beginning and end of the process which supplies the content of the novel, thus become significant landmarks along a clearly mapped road. The novel in itself and for itself is by no means bound to the natural beginning and end of life—to birth and death; yet by the points at which it begins and ends, it indicates the only essential segment of life, that segment which is determined by the central problem, and it touches upon whatever lies before or after that segment only in perspective and only as it relates to that problem; it tends to unfold its full epic totality only within that span of life which is essential to it.

When the beginning and the end of this segment of life do not coincide with those of a human life, this merely shows that the biographical form is oriented towards ideas: the development of a man is still the thread upon which the whole world of the novel is strung and along which it unrolls, but now this development acquires significance only because it is typical of that system of ideas and experienced ideals which regulatively determines the inner and outer world of the novel.

Wilhelm Meister's existence in literature stretches from the point at which his crisis in face of the given circumstances of his life becomes acute to the point at which he finds the profession which is appropriate to his essence; but the underlying principle of this biographical structure is the same as in Pontoppidan's *Hans im Glück*, which begins with the hero's first significant childhood experience and ends with his death. In either case the stylisation differs radically from that of the epic. In the epic, the central figure and its significant adventures are a mass organised in itself and for itself, so that the beginning and the end mean something quite different there, something essentially less important: they are moments of great intensity, homogeneous with other points which are the high points of the whole; they never signify anything more than the commencement or the resolution of great tensions.

Once more Dante's position is a special one; in Dante, principles of structuration which tend towards the novel are re-transformed back into the epic. The beginning and the end in Dante represent the decisive points of essential life, and everything that can acquire significance by having meaning conferred upon it takes place between those points; before the beginning there lay unredeemable chaos, after the end lies the no longer threatened certainty of redemption. But what is contained between the beginning and the end escapes the biographical categories of the process: it is the *eternally existent becoming* of ecstasy; whatever the novel might have taken hold of and structured is, in

Dante, condemned to absolute inessentiality by the paramount significance of this experience.

The novel comprises the essence of its totality between the beginning and the end, and thereby raises an individual to the infinite heights of one who must create an entire world through his experience and who must maintain that world in equilibrium—heights which no epic individual, not even Dante's, could reach, because the epic individual owed his significance to the grace accorded him, not to his pure individuality. But just because the novel can only comprise the individual in this way, he becomes a mere instrument, and his central position in the work means only that he is particularly well suited to reveal a certain problematic of life.

5

The Historico-philosophical Conditioning of the Novel and its Significance

THE COMPOSITION of the novel is the paradoxical fusion of heterogeneous and discrete components into an organic whole which is then abolished over and over again. The relationships which create cohesion between the abstract components are abstractly pure and formal, and the ultimate unifying principle therefore has to be the ethic of the creative subjectivity, an ethic which the content reveals. But because this ethic must surmount itself so that the author's normative objectivity may be realised, and because it cannot, when all is said and done, completely penetrate the objects of form-giving, and therefore cannot completely rid itself of its subjectivity and so appear as the immanent meaning of the objective world—because of this, it needs a new ethical self-correction, again determined by the work's content, in order to achieve the 'tact' which will create a proper balance. This interaction of two ethical complexes, their duality as to form and their unity in being given form, is the content of irony, which is the normative mentality of the novel. The novel is condemned to great complexity by the structure of its given nature. What happens to an idea in the world of reality need not become the object of dialectical reflexion in every kind of literary creation in which an idea is given form as reality. The relationship between idea and reality can be dealt with by means of purely sensuous form-giving, and then no empty space or distance is left between the two which would have to be filled with the author's consciousness and wisdom. Wisdom can be expressed through the act of form-giving: it can conceal itself behind the forms and does not necessarily have to surmount itself, as irony, in the work.

For the creative individual's reflexion, the novelist's ethic vis-à-vis the content, is a double one. His reflexion consists of giving form to what happens to the idea in real life, of describing the actual nature of this process and of evaluating and considering its reality. This reflexion, however, in turn becomes an object for reflexion; it is itself only an ideal, only subjective and postulative; it, too, has a certain destiny in a reality which is alien to it; and this destiny, now purely reflexive and contained within the narrator himself, must also be given form.

The need for reflexion is the deepest melancholy of every great and genuine novel. Through it, the writer's naïvety suffers extreme violence and is changed into its opposite. (This is only another way of saying that pure reflexion is profoundly inartistic.) And the hard-won equalisation, the unstable balance of mutually surmounting reflexions—the second naïvety, which is the novelist's objectivity—is only a formal substitute for the first: it makes form-giving possible and it rounds off the form, but the very manner in which it does so points eloquently at the sacrifice that has had to be made, at the paradise forever lost, sought and never found. This vain search and then the resignation with which it is abandoned make the circle that completes the form.

The novel is the form of mature virility: its author has lost the poet's radiant youthful faith 'that destiny and soul are twin names for a single concept' (Novalis); and the deeper and more painful his need to set this most essential creed of all literature as a demand against life, the more deeply and painfully he must learn to understand that it is only a demand and not an effective reality. This insight, this irony, is directed both at his heroes, who, in their poetically necessary youthfulness, are destroyed by trying to turn his faith into reality, and against his own wisdom, which has been forced to see the uselessness of the struggle and the final victory of reality. Indeed, the irony is a double one in both directions. It extends

not only to the profound hopelessness of the struggle but also
to the still more profound hopelessness of its abandonment
—the pitiful failure of the intention to adapt to a world
which is a stranger to ideals, to abandon the unreal ideality
of the soul for the sake of achieving mastery over reality. And
whilst irony depicts reality as victorious, it reveals not only
that reality is as nothing in face of its defeated opponent,
not only that the victory of reality can never be a final one,
that it will always, again and again, be challenged by new
rebellions of the idea, but also that reality owes its advantage
not so much to its own strength, which is too crude and
directionless to maintain the advantage, as to the inner
(although necessary) problematic of the soul weighed down
by its ideals.

The melancholy of the adult state arises from our dual,
conflicting experience that, on the one hand, our absolute,
youthful confidence in an inner voice has diminished or died,
and, on the other hand, that the outside world to which we
now devote ourselves in our desire to learn its ways and
dominate it will never speak to us in a voice that will clearly
tell us our way and determine our goal. The heroes of youth
are guided by the gods: whether what awaits them at the
end of the road are the embers of annihilation or the joys
of success, or both at once, they never walk alone, they are
always led. Hence the deep certainty with which they
proceed: they may weep and mourn, forsaken by everyone,
on a desert island, they may stumble to the very gates of hell
in desperate blindness, yet an atmosphere of security always
surrounds them; a god always plots the hero's paths and
always walks ahead of him.

Fallen gods, and gods whose kingdom is not yet,
become demons; their power is effective and alive, but it no
longer penetrates the world, or does not yet do so: the world
has a coherence of meaning, a causality, which is incomprehensible to the vital, effective force of a god-become-demon;

from the demon's viewpoint, the affairs of such a world appear purely senseless. The demon's power remains effective because it cannot be overthrown; the passing of the old god supports the being of the new; and for this reason the one possesses the same valency of reality (in the sphere of the only essential being, which is metaphysical being) as the other. 'It was not divine,' Goethe wrote about the daemonic, 'for it seemed irrational; it was not human, for it had no reason; not devilish, for it was beneficent; not angelic, for it often allowed room for malice. It resembled the accidental, for it was without consequence; it looked like providence, for it hinted at hidden connections. Everything that restricts us seemed permeable by it; it seemed to arrange at will the necessary elements of our existence; it contracted time, it expanded space. It seemed at ease only in the impossible, and it thrust the possible from itself with contempt.'

But there is an essential aspiration of the soul which is con-cerned only with the essential, no matter where it comes from or where it leads; there is a nostalgia of the soul when the longing for home is so violent that the soul must, with blind impetuousness, take the first path that seems to lead there; and so powerful is this yearning that it can always pursue its road to the end. For such a soul, every road leads to the essence—leads home—for to this soul its selfhood *is* its home. That is why tragedy knows no real difference between God and demon, whereas, if a demon enters the domain of the epic at all, he has to be a powerless, defeated higher being, a deposed divinity. Tragedy destroys the hierarchy of the higher worlds; in it there is no God and no demon, for the outside world is only the occasion for the soul to find itself, for the hero to become a hero; in itself and for itself, it is neither perfectly nor imperfectly penetrated by meaning; it is a tangle of blind happenings, indifferent to objective existing forms of meaning. But the soul transforms every happening into destiny, and the soul alone does this for everyone. Only when the tragedy is over, when the dramatic meaning has become transcendent, do gods and demons appear on the stage; it is only in the drama of grace that the *tabula rasa* of the higher world is filled once more with superior and subordinate figures.

The novel is the epic of a world that has been abandoned by God. The novel hero's psychology is demonic; the objectivity of the novel is the mature man's knowledge that meaning can never quite penetrate reality, but that, without meaning, reality would disintegrate into the nothingness of inessentiality. These are merely different ways of saying the same thing. They define the productive limits of the possibilities of the novel—limits which are drawn from within—and, at the same time, they define the historico-philosophical moment at which great novels become possible, at which they grow into a symbol of the essential thing that needs to be said. The mental attitude of the novel is virile maturity, and the characteristic structure of its matter is discreteness, the separation between interiority and adventure.

'I go to prove my soul,' says Browning's Paracelsus, and if the marvellous line is out of place it is only because it is spoken by a dramatic hero. The dramatic hero knows no adventure, for, through the force of his attained soul that is hallowed by destiny, the event which should have been his adventure becomes destiny upon the merest contact with that soul, becomes a simple occasion for him to prove himself, a simple excuse for disclosing what was prefigured in the act of his attaining the soul. The dramatic hero knows no interiority, for interiority is the product of the antagonistic duality of soul and world, the agonising distance between psyche and soul; and the tragic hero has attained his soul and therefore does not know any hostile reality: everything exterior is, for him, merely an expression of a predetermined and adequate destiny. Therefore the dramatic hero does not set out to prove himself: he is a hero because his inner security is given *a priori*, beyond the reach of any test or proof; the destiny-forming event is, for him, only a symbolic objectivation, a profound and dignified ceremony.

(The essential inner stylelessness of modern drama, and of Ibsen in particular, derives from the fact that his major figures have to be tested, that they sense within themselves the distance between themselves and their soul, and, in their desperate desire to pass the tests with which events confront them, try to bridge that distance. The heroes of modern drama experience the preconditions of drama; the drama itself unfolds in the process of stylisation which the dramatist should have completed, as a phenomenological precondition of his work, before beginning to write it.)

The novel tells of the adventure of interiority; the content of the novel is the story of the soul that goes to find itself, that seeks adventures in order to be proved and tested by them, and, by proving itself, to find its own essence. The inner security of the epic world excludes adventure in this essential sense: the heroes of the epic live through a whole variety of adventures, but the fact that they will pass the test, both inwardly and outwardly, is never in doubt; the world-dominating gods must always triumph over the demons ('the divinities of impediment', as Indian mythology calls them). Hence the passivity of the epic hero that Goethe and Schiller insisted on: the adventures that fill and embellish his life are the form taken by the objective and extensive totality of the world; he himself is only the luminous centre around which this unfolded totality revolves, the inwardly most immobile point of the world's rhythmic movement. By contrast, the novel hero's passivity is not a necessity; it characterises the hero's relationship to his soul and to the outside world. The novel hero does not have to be passive: that is why his passivity has a specific psychological and sociological nature and represents a distinct type in the structural possibilities of the novel.

The novel hero's psychology is the field of action of the demonic. Biological and sociological life has a profound tendency to remain within its own immanence; men want only to live, structures want to remain intact; and because of the remoteness, the absence of an effective God, the indolent self-complacency of this quietly decaying life would be the only power in the world if men did not sometimes fall prey to the power of the demon and overreach themselves in ways that have no reason and cannot be explained by reason, challenging all the psychological or sociological foundations of their existence. Then, suddenly, the God-forsakenness of the world reveals itself as a lack of substance, as an irrational mixture of density and permeability. What previously seemed to be very solid crumbles like dry clay at the first contact with a man possessed by a demon, and the empty transparence behind which attractive landscapes were previously to be seen is suddenly transformed into a glass wall against which men beat in vain, like bees against a window, incapable of breaking through, incapable of understanding that the way is barred.

The writer's irony is a negative mysticism to be found in times without a god. It is an attitude of *docta ignorantia* towards meaning, a portrayal of the kindly and malicious workings of the demons, a refusal to comprehend more than the mere fact of these workings; and in it there is the deep certainty, expressible only by form-giving, that through not-desiring-to-know and not-being-able-to-know he has truly encountered, glimpsed and grasped the ultimate, true substance, the present, non-existent God. This is why irony is the objectivity of the novel.

'To what extent are a writer's characters objective?' asks Hebbel. 'To the extent that man is free in his relationship to God.' A mystic is free when he has renounced himself and is totally dissolved in God; a hero is free when, proud as Lucifer, he has achieved perfection in himself and out of himself; when, for the sake of his soul's free activity, he has banished all half-measures from the world whose ruler he has become because of his fall. Normative man has achieved freedom in his relationship to God because the lofty norms of his actions and of his substantial ethic are rooted in the existence of the all-perfecting God, are rooted in the idea of redemption, because they remain untouched in their innermost essence by whoever dominates the present, be he God or demon. But the realisation of the normative in the soul or the work cannot be separated from its substratum which is the present (in the historico-philosophical sense), without jeopardising its most specific strength, its constitutive relatedness with its object. Even the mystic who aspires to the experience of a final and unique Godhead outside all formed concepts of a God, and who achieves such an experience, is still tied to the present God of his time; and in so far as his experience is perfected and becomes a work, it is perfected within the categories prescribed by the historico-philosophical position of the world's clock. Thus his freedom is subject to a double categorical dialectic, a theoretical and a historico-philosophical one; that part of it which is the most specific essence of freedom—the constitutive relation to redemption—remains inexpressible; everything that can be expressed and given form bears witness to this double servitude.

The detour by way of speech to silence, by way of category to essence, is unavoidable: when the historical categories are not sufficiently developed, the wish to achieve immediate silence must inevitably lead to mere stuttering. But when the form is perfectly achieved, the writer is free in relation to God because in such a form, and only in it, God himself becomes the substratum of form-giving, homogeneous with and equivalent to all the other normatively given elements of form, and is completely embraced by its system of categories. The writer's existence and its very quality are determined by the normative relationship which he as the form-giver has with the structural forms—by the value technically assigned to him for structuring and articulating the work. But such subsuming of God under the technical concept of the 'material authenticity' of a form reveals the double face of an artistic creation and shows its true place in the order of metaphysically significant works: such perfect technical immanence has as its precondition a constitutive relationship (which is normatively, but not psychologically, a preliminary one) to ultimate transcendent existence. The reality-creating, transcendental form can only come into being when a true transcendence has become immanent within it. An empty immanence, which is anchored only in the writer's experience and not, at the same time, in his return to the home of all things, is merely the immanence of a surface that covers up the cracks but is incapable of retaining this immanence and must become a surface riddled with holes.

For the novel, irony consists in this freedom of the writer in his relationship to God, the transcendental condition of the objectivity of form-giving. Irony, with intuitive double vision, can see where God is to be found in a world abandoned by God; irony sees the lost, utopian home of the idea that has become an ideal, and yet at the same time it understands that the ideal is subjectively and psychologically conditioned, because that is its only possible form of existence; irony, itself demonic, apprehends the demon that is within the subject as a metasubjective essentiality, and therefore, when it speaks of the adventures of errant souls in an inessential, empty reality, it intuitively speaks of past gods and gods that are to come; irony has to seek the only world that is adequate to it along the *via dolorosa* of interiority, but is doomed never to find it there; irony gives form to the malicious satisfaction of God the creator at the failure of man's weak rebellions against his mighty, yet worthless creation and, at the same time, to the inexpressible suffering of God the redeemer at his inability to re-enter that world. Irony, the self-surmounting of a subjectivity that has gone as far as it was possible to go, is the highest freedom that can be achieved in a world without God. That is why it is not only the sole possible *a priori* condition for a true, totality-creating objectivity but also why it makes that totality—the novel—the representative art-form of our age: because the structural categories of the novel constitutively coincide with the world as it is today.

II

ATTEMPT AT A TYPOLOGY OF
THE NOVEL FORM

I

Abstract Idealism

THE ABANDONMENT of the world by God manifests itself in the incommensurability of soul and work, of interiority and adventure—in the absence of a transcendental 'place' allotted to human endeavour. There are, roughly speaking, two types of such incommensurability: either the world is narrower or it is broader than the outside world assigned to it as the arena and substratum of its actions.

In the first case, the demonic character of the problematic individual setting out on his adventurous course is more clearly visible than in the second case, but, at the same time, his inner problematic is less sharply obvious; his failure in the face of reality looks at first glance like a merely outward failure. The demonism of the narrowing of the soul is the demonism of abstract idealism. It is the mentality which chooses the direct, straight path towards the realisation of the ideal; which, dazzled by the demon, forgets the existence of any distance between ideal and idea, between psyche and soul; which, with the most authentic and unshakeable faith, concludes that the idea, because it *should be*, necessarily *must be*, and, because reality does not satisfy this *a priori* demand, thinks that reality is bewitched by evil demons and that the spell can be broken and reality can be redeemed either by finding a magic password or by courageously fighting the evil forces.

The structure-determining problematic of this type of hero consists, therefore, in the complete absence of an inner problematic and, consequently, in the complete lack of any transcendental sense of space, i.e. of the ability to experience distances as realities.

G   97

Achilles or Odysseus, Dante or Arjuna—precisely because
they are guided along their paths by gods—realise that if
they lacked this guidance, if they were without divine help,
they would be powerless and helpless in the face of mighty
enemies. The relationship between the objective and subjective worlds is therefore maintained in adequate balance:
the hero is rightly conscious of the superiority of the opposing outside world; yet despite this innermost modesty he
can triumph in the end because his lesser strength is guided
to victory by the highest power in the world; the forces
of the imaginary and the real correspond with one another;
the victories and defeats are not contradictory to either the
actual or the ideal world order.

When this instinctive sense of distance, which is an
essential factor in the complete life-immanence, in the 'health'
of the epic, is lacking, the relationship between the subjective
and the objective worlds becomes paradoxical; because the
active soul, the soul that matters from the point of view of
the epic, is narrowed, the world—as the substratum of its
actions—likewise becomes narrower for that soul than it is
in reality. But since this reduction of the world and every
action which follows from it and which is aimed only at
the reduced world must fall short of the real centre of the
outside world, and since, too, such an attitude is of necessity
a subjective one, leaving the essence of the world untouched
and offering only a distorted image of it, all that opposes the
soul must come from sources which are completely heterogeneous from it. Thus action and opposition have neither scope
nor quality—neither reality nor orientation—in common.
Their relationship to one another is not one of true struggle
but only of a grotesque failure to meet, or an equally grotesque
clash conditioned by reciprocal misunderstandings. The
narrowing of the soul of which we speak is brought about
by its demonic obsession by an existing idea which it posits
as the only, the most ordinary reality. The content and in-

tensity of the actions which follows from this obsession therefore elevate the soul into the most genuinely sublime regions whilst at the same time accentuating and confirming the grotesque contradictions between the imagined and the real. And this is the action of the novel. The novel's discrete-heterogeneous nature is revealed here with maximum vividness; the sphere of the soul—of psychology—and the sphere of action no longer have anything whatsoever in common.

Furthermore, in neither of the two spheres is there an element of immanent progress or development, either within itself or arising from relationships with the other. The soul is at rest in the transcendent existence it has achieved on the far side of all problems; no doubts, no search, no despair can arise within it so as to take it out of itself and set it in motion. Its grotesque, vain struggles to realise itself in the outside world will not really touch such a soul; nothing can shake it in its inner certitude, because it is imprisoned in its safe world—because it is incapable of experiencing anything. The complete absence of an inwardly experienced problematic transforms such a soul into pure activity. Because it is at rest within its essential existence, every one of its impulses becomes an action aimed at the outside. The life of a person with such a soul becomes an uninterrupted series of adventures which he himself has chosen. He throws himself into them because life means nothing more to him than the successful passing of tests. His unquestioning, concentrated interiority forces him to translate that interiority—which he considers to be the average, everyday nature of the real world—into actions; in respect of this aspect of his soul he is incapable of any contemplation; he lacks any inclination or possibility of inward-turned activity. He has to be an adventurer. Yet the world he is obliged to choose as the arena for his adventures is a curious mixture of the richly organic, which is completely alien to ideas, and of those self-same ideas (the ideas which lead their purely transcendent life inside his soul) petrified into social convention. This is what makes it possible for his actions to be spontaneous and ideological at the same time: the world he finds is not only full of life, but also full of the semblance of the very life which exists inside him as the only essential life. However, this capacity of the world to be misunderstood is also the reason why he can so grotesquely act at cross-purposes with it: the semblance of an idea collapses in face of the absurd, petrified ideal, and the real nature of the existing world, the self-maintaining, organic life that is alien to all ideas, assumes its appropriate all-dominant position.

It is here that the ungodly, demonic character of such an obsession is most clearly revealed, but so also is its likewise demonic, confusing and fascinating resemblance to the divine. The hero's soul is at rest, rounded and complete within itself like a work of art or a divinity; but this mode of being can only express itself in the outside world by means of inadequate adventures which contain no counter-force within them precisely because the hero is so maniacally imprisoned in himself; and this isolation, which makes the soul resemble a work of art, also separates it from all outside reality and from all those other areas of the soul which have not been seized by the demon. Thus a maximum of inwardly attained meaning becomes a maximum of senselessness and the sublime turns to madness, to monomania.

Such a structure of the soul completely atomises the mass of possible actions. Because of the purely reflexive nature of the soul's interiority, outside reality remains quite untouched by it, and reveals itself 'as it really is' only as an opposition to every one of the hero's actions. Nevertheless this outside reality is no more than a sluggish, formless, meaningless mass entirely lacking any capacity for planned and consistent counter-action, and the hero in his demonic search for adventure arbitrarily and disconnectedly selects those moments of this 'reality' which he thinks most suitable for 'proving himself'. Thus the hero's psychological rigidity and the mass of action which has been atomised into a series of isolated adventures mutually determine one another and, as a result, clearly reveal the risk inherent in this type of novel: the risk of 'bad' abstraction, 'bad' infinity.

The reason why this danger is avoided in *Don Quixote*, the immortal objectivation of this type of hero, lies not only in Cervantes' genius and the extraordinary tact with which he overcomes the danger by means of the impenetrably deep yet radiantly sensuous interweaving of divinity with madness in Don Quixote's soul, but also in the historico-philosophical moment at which the work was written. It is more than a mere accident of history that *Don Quixote* was intended as a parody of the chivalrous novels, and its relation to them is more than an essayistic one. The chivalrous novel had succumbed to the fate of every epic that wants to maintain and perpetuate a form by purely formal means after the transcendental conditions for its existence have already been condemned by the historico-philosophical dialectic. The chivalrous novel had lost its roots in transcendent being, and the forms, which no longer had any immanent function, withered away, became abstract, because their strength, which had been intended for the creation of objects, was exhausted by its own objectlessness. The great epic was replaced by entertainment literature. Yet behind the empty shell of these dead forms there had once been a pure and genuine major art form, even if a problematic one: the chivalrous epic of the Middle Ages.

We have here the curious case of a novel form existing in a period whose absolute belief in God really encouraged the epic. It is the great paradox of the Christian universe that the fragmentariness, the normatively imperfect nature of earthly life, its enslavement by error and sin, is opposed by the eternally present theodicy of the life of the beyond. Dante succeeded in capturing this dual world-totality in the purely epic form of the *Divina Commedia*. Other epic writers, who remained on earth, had to leave the transcendent in a state of artificially untouched transcendence and so could only create sentimentally conceived life-totalities which were desired but which lacked any existing immanence of meaning. They created novels, not epics.

The unique quality of these novels, their dreamlike beauty and magic grace, consists in the fact that all the seeking which is in them is, after all, only a semblance of seeking. Every errant step of their heroes is guided and made safe by an unfathomable, metaformal grace; distance, losing its objective reality, is turned into a darkly beautiful ornament, and the leap necessary to bridge it is turned into a dance-like gesture—both distance and leap are transformed into purely decorative elements. These novels are in substance vast fairy-tales, for in them transcendence is not captured, made immanent and absorbed in the object-creating, transcendental form, but remains in its undiluted transcendence; the shadow of transcendence decoratively fills the cracks of earthly life and turns the matter of life—because of the dynamic homogeneity of every true work of art—into a substance that is likewise woven out of shadows. In the Homeric epics the omnipotence of the purely human category of life embraced both men and gods and made purely human beings out of them. Here it is the elusive divine principle that dominates, with the same omnipotence, both the life of man and its need to go outside itself, to complement itself; and this creates a flatness, robs the human characters of all relief, transforms them into pure surface.

The safe, rounded irrationality of the entire cosmos, as reflected in these novels, makes the glimpsed shadow of God appear demonic: he cannot be comprehended and fitted into some kind of order from the perspective of earthly life, and therefore he cannot reveal himself as God. Nor is it possible, as it was in Dante—because these novels are centred on earthly life—to use God as the starting point for finding and uncovering the constitutive unity of all existence. The chivalrous novels against which *Don Quixote* was in the first place a polemic and which it parodied had lost the necessary transcendent relationship, and given this loss—unless everything, as in Ariosto, was to become pure, ironically elegant play—their mysterious and fairy-tale like surfaces were bound to degenerate into banal superficiality. Cervantes' creative criticism of the triviality of the chivalrous novel leads us once more to the historico-philosophical sources of this genre. The subjectively incomprehensible, objectively secure existence of the idea is transformed into a subjectively clear, fanatically maintained existence, lacking any objective relationship. The God who, because of the inadequacy of the material enfolding him, could only appear as a demon, actually becomes a demon, arrogating to himself the role of God, in a world forsaken by providence and lacking transcendental orientation. This world is the same one which God had previously transformed into a dangerous but wonderful magic garden; now, turned into prose by evil demons, this world yearns to be transformed back again into a magic garden by faithful heroes. That which, in the fairy-tale, had only to be guarded against so as to preserve the beneficent spell, here becomes positive action, becomes a struggle for the existing paradise of a fairy-tale reality which awaits the redeeming word.

Thus the first great novel of world literature stands at the beginning of the time when the Christian God began to forsake the world; when man became lonely and could find meaning and substance only in his own soul, whose home was nowhere; when the world, released from its paradoxical anchorage in a beyond that is truly present, was abandoned to its immanent meaninglessness; when the power of what is—reinforced by the utopian links, now degraded to mere existence—had grown to incredible magnitude and was waging a furious, apparently aimless struggle against the new forces which were as yet weak and incapable of revealing themselves or penetrating the world. Cervantes lived in the period of the last, great and desperate mysticism, the period of a fanatical attempt to renew the dying religion from within; a period of a new view of the world rising up in mystical forms; the last period of truly lived but already dis-oriented, tentative, sophisticated, occult aspirations.

It was the period of the demons let loose, a period of great confusion of values in the midst of an as yet unchanged value system. And Cervantes, the faithful Christian and naïvely loyal patriot, creatively exposed the deepest essence of this demonic problematic: the purest heroism is bound to become grotesque, the strongest faith is bound to become madness, when the ways leading to the transcendental home have become impassable; reality does not have to correspond to subjective evidence, however genuine and heroic. The profound melancholy of the historical process, of the passing of time, speaks through this work, telling us that even a con-tent and an attitude which are eternal must lose their mean-ing when their time is past: that time brushes aside even the eternal. *Don Quixote* is the first great battle of interiority against the prosaic vulgarity of outward life, and the only battle in which interiority succeeded, not only to emerge unblemished from the fray, but even to transmit some of the radiance of its triumphant, though admittedly self-ironising, poetry to its victorious opponent.

Don Quixote—like almost any truly great novel—had to remain the only important objectivation of its type. This particular mixture of poetry and irony, the sublime and the grotesque, divinity and monomania, was so strongly bound up with the historical moment that the same type of mental structure was bound to manifest itself differently at other times and was never again to reach the same epic significance.

The adventure novels which took over its purely artistic form became just as devoid of ideas as its immediate predecessors, the chivalrous novels. They, too, lost the only fruitful tension—a transcendental one—and either replaced it by a purely social tension or simply found the motivation for action in a spirit of adventure for adventure's sake. In either case, and despite the genuinely great talent of some of the writers involved, an ultimate triviality, an ever-increasing similarity between the great novel and the entertainment novel, and the final merging of the two could not be avoided. As the world becomes more and more prosaic, as the active demons withdraw from the world leaving the arena free to the dull opposition of an inchoate mass to any kind of interiority, the demonically narrowed soul faces a new dilemma: either it must give up all relationship to life or it must lose its immediate roots in the true world of ideas.

The great dramas of German idealism chose the first path. Abstract idealism lost even the most inadequate relationship to life; in order to come out of its subjectivity and prove itself in struggle and defeat, it needed the pure essential sphere of the drama: interiority and the world had come to be at such cross-purposes with one another that their situation could be given as a form of totality only as part of a dramatic reality specially designed and constructed to that end. Kleist's *Michael Kohlhaas*, artistically a major work, shows to what degree the situation of the time demanded that the hero's psychology should become a matter of purely individual pathology, so that the epic form had to become that of the novella. In this form, as in any dramatic form-giving, the profound interpenetration of the sublime and the grotesque must give place to the purely sublime: the monomania is so acute, the abstraction so extreme, the idealism inevitably becomes so thin, so contentless, so generalised, that the characters move very near the frontier of unconscious comedy and the smallest attempt at irony would banish the sublime and transform them into embarrassingly comic figures. (Brand, Stockmann and Gregers Werle are cautionary examples of this possibility.) Marquis Posa, the true descendant of Don Quixote, lives in an entirely different form from his ancestor's and, in terms of art, the problems of the destiny of these two souls which are so alike are utterly different.

If the narrowing of the soul is a purely psychological phenomenon, if it has lost any visible relation to the existence of the world of ideas, then it has also lost the ability to be the sustaining centre of an epic totality. In this case the inadequacy of the relation between the hero and the outside world is further intensified, but in addition to the *actual* inadequacy (which in *Don Quixote* has been merely the grotesque counterpart of an adequacy that was continually demanded and insisted upon as *ideal*), there is also an inadequacy *at the level of ideas*: the contact between the hero and the outside world becomes a purely peripheral one: the hero is merely a necessary secondary figure adorning a totality and contributing to its construction, but remaining only a brick in the edifice, never its centre. The consequent danger, artistically speaking, is that the centre which is now needed has to be something that has meaning and value, but not something which transcends the immanence of life. This change in transcendental attitude means in terms of artistic method that the source of humour is no longer the same as that of poetry and the sublime. Grotesquely depicted characters either become innocuously comic, or else the narrowing of their souls, their all-devouring concentration upon a single point of existence, which no longer has anything to do with the world of ideas, produces pure demonism, and the characters, however humorously treated, become representatives of the 'bad' principle or of the pure absence of ideas.

This negativity of the central characters requires a positive counterweight and, most unhappily for the modern humorous novel, this 'positive' counterweight can be nothing else but the objectivation of the bourgeois concept of decent behaviour. A true relation between this 'positive' element and the world of ideas would destroy the immanence of meaning in life, and, with it, the novel form. Cervantes (and, among his successors, perhaps Sterne) was able to create such immanence only by blending the sublime with the humorous, the narrowing of the soul with its relationship to transcendence. This is the artistic reason why Dickens' novels, so marvellously rich in comic characters, seem in the end so flat and moralistic. He had to make his heroes come to terms, without conflict, with the bourgeois society of his time and, for the sake of poetic effect, to surround the qualities needed for this purpose with a false, or anyway inadequate, poetic glow. Gogol's *Dead Souls* had to remain a fragment for probably the same reason: it was impossible from the start to find a 'positive' counterweight to Chichikov, a character who is, artistically speaking, wonderfully fertile and well-realised, yet undeniably 'negative'. In order to create a real totality such as Gogol's authentically epic intention demanded, a balance was absolutely essential; without it, the novel could not achieve epic objectivity or epic reality: it would remain a purely subjective work or a satirical tract.

The outside world today has become so exclusively conventional that everything, positive or negative, humorous or poetic, can take place only within the sphere of convention. The demonically humorous is nothing other than a distorted exaggeration of certain aspects of convention or its immanent (and therefore in turn conventional) denial and rejection; and the 'positive' is a coming-to-terms with it, the semblance of an organic life within limits clearly laid down by convention.

(This historico-philosophically determined conventionality of the modern humorous novel should not be confused with the form-determined and therefore timeless conventions of dramatic comedy. In the latter, certain conventional forms of social life are merely the formal-symbolic conclusions of the rounded essential sphere of the drama. When all the major characters with the exception of the unmasked hypocrites and villains marry one another at the end of the great comedies, this is just as much a symbolic ceremony as the hero's death at the end of tragedy; both are no more than symbols indicating the drawing of a boundary, the drawing of the sharp outline required by the sculptural essentiality of the drama. It is a characteristic fact that as the conventionality of real life and of the epic increases, so the endings of comedies become less and less conventional. *The Broken Jug* and *The Inspector-General* can still use the old unmasking technique, but *The Parisienne*—not to mention Hauptmann's or Shaw's comedies—is as contourless and unfinished as today's tragedies, which do not end with the hero's death.)

Balzac chose a completely different path towards epic immanence. For him the subjective-psychological demonism which is characteristic of his work is an ultimate reality, the principle of all essential action which objectivises itself in heroic deeds; its inadequate relation to the outside world is intensified to the utmost, but this intensification has a purely immanent counterweight: the outside world is a purely human one and is essentially peopled by human beings with similar mental structures, although with completely different orientations and contents. As a result, this demonic inadequacy, this endless series of incidents in which souls are fatally at cross-purposes with one another, becomes the essence of reality, and we obtain that strange, boundless, immeasurable mass of interweaving destinies and lonely souls which is the unique feature of Balzac's novels. By this paradoxical homogeneity of the material of these novels, which in turn results from the extreme heterogeneity of its constituent elements, an immanence of meaning is rescued. The danger of an abstract, 'bad' infinity is avoided by a great concentration of events (as in a novella) and a genuinely epic significance is thus attained.

However, this triumph of form occurs only in each individual novel, not in *The Human Comedy* as a whole. True, the prerequisite for it is there: the magnificent unity of the work's all-embracing material. This unity is not merely realised by means of the repeated appearances and disappearances of individual characters in the infinite chaos of the different stories; it also takes a form which is completely adequate to the innermost essence of this material, that of chaotic, demonic irrationality. And the content which fills this unity is that of the authentic great epic—the totality of a world. But ultimately this totality is not born purely out of the form: what makes the whole truly a whole is, in the end, only the effective experience of a common basis of life and the recognition that this experience corresponds to the essence of life as lived at that moment. Only the details are epically formed, the whole is merely fitted together; the 'bad' infinity, surmounted in every individual part, defeats the whole as a unified epic work: the totality rests on principles which do not belong to the epic form, on mood and insight, not on actions and heroes, and so the totality is not complete and rounded in itself. None of the parts, seen from the viewpoint of the whole, possesses an organic necessity of existence; if it were not there at all, the whole would not suffer; conversely, any number of new parts might be added and no evidence of inner completeness would prove them superfluous. The totality here is the sense of a life order, which we feel as a great lyric backdrop behind each individual story; it is not problematic, it has not been achieved by difficult struggles as in the great novels. The totality of *The Human Comedy* as a whole, with its essentially lyrical nature that belongs outside the epic, is naïve and unproblematic. And if this totality is inadequate for the novel, it is even less adequate for the epic.

A static psychology is the common feature of all these attempts at form-giving; the narrowing of the soul is a given, unchangeable, abstract *a priori* condition. It was natural, therefore, that the nineteenth-century novel with its tendencies towards psychological dynamism and psychologistic solutions should depart increasingly from this type and should seek the causes of the inadequacy between soul and reality in quite other directions. Only one great novel, Pontoppidan's *Hans im Glück*, represents an attempt to treat this type of soul structure centrally and to portray it through movement and development. Pontoppidan's manner of posing the problem leads to a completely new method of composition: the point of departure, the subject's completely secure bond with the transcendent essence, becomes the final goal, and the demonic tendency of the soul to divorce itself completely from anything that does not correspond to this *a priori* condition becomes a real tendency. Whereas in *Don Quixote* the basis of all the hero's adventures was his inner certainty and the world's inadequate attitude towards it, so that the role of the demonic became a positive, dynamic one, here the unity between basis and end-goal is concealed, the divergence between soul and reality becomes mysterious and apparently quite irrational; the demonic narrowing of the soul manifests itself only negatively, by the hero having to abandon everything he achieves because it is never what he wants, because it is broader, more empirical, more life-like than what his soul set out to seek. Whereas in *Don Quixote* the completion of the life cycle is the same adventure repeated over and over again in different ways and extended until it becomes the all-containing centre of the totality, here the movement of life shows a definite and unmistakable progression towards the purity of a soul that has attained itself, learning from its adventures that only it alone, rigidly confined within itself, can correspond to its deepest, all-dominating instinct; that the soul is bound to be imprisoned and ultimately destroyed in a world which is alien to its essence: that every refusal to seize a conquered piece of reality is really a victory, a step towards the conquest of a self freed from illusions.

Pontoppidan's irony lies in the fact that he lets his hero succeed all the time, but shows that a demonic power forces him to regard everything he has gained as worthless and inessential and to throw it away as soon as he has gained it. The curious inner tension of the book is due to the fact that the meaning of this negative demonism is revealed only at the end, when the hero achieves complete resignation, thus giving restrospective immanence of meaning to his whole life. The revealed transcendence of this ending and its evident pre-stabilised harmony with the soul give an appearance of necessity to all the confusions that preceded it; indeed, seen from the end, the dynamic relationship between the soul and the world is reversed; it looks as though the hero had always remained unchanged, quietly watching the passing events from within himself; as though the entire action consisted merely in removing the veils in which his soul was wrapped. The dynamic nature of psychology is thus shown to be only apparently dynamic, but not until— and this is where Pontoppidan's great mastery lies—it has rendered possible a journey through a really vital and dynamic life-totality by its semblance of movement. This explains the isolated position of Pontoppidan's work among modern novels, its strict insistence upon action which is reminiscent of novels of the past, its rejection of mere psychology, and —in terms of mood—the profound difference between the resignation which is felt at the end of this novel and the disappointed romanticism of other contemporary works.

2

The Romanticism of Disillusionment

IN THE nineteenth century novel, the other type of the necessarily inadequate relation between soul and reality became the more important one: the inadequacy that is due to the soul's being wider and larger than the destinies which life has to offer it. The decisive structural difference is that here we are not dealing with an abstract *a priori* condition on the face of life, a condition which seeks to realise itself in action and therefore provokes conflicts with the outside world which make up the story of the novel; but rather a purely interior reality which is full of content and more or less complete in itself enters into competition with the reality of the outside world, leads a rich and animated life of its own and, with spontaneous self-confidence, regards itself as the only true reality, the essence of the world: and the failure of every attempt to realise this equality is the subject of the work.

Thus we have here a concrete, qualitative *a priori* attitude vis-à-vis the world—a matter of content, a struggle between two worlds, not a struggle between reality and a general *a priori* state. But this makes the divergence between interiority and the outside world even stronger. When the interiority is like a cosmos, it is self-sufficient, at rest within itself. Whereas abstract idealism, in order to exist at all, had to translate itself into action, had to enter into conflict with the outside world, here the possibility of escape does not seem excluded from the start. A life which is capable of producing all its content out of itself can be rounded and perfect even if it never enters into contact with the alien reality outside. Whereas, therefore, an excessive, totally uninhibited activity towards the outside world was characteristic of the psychological structure of abstract idealism, here the tendency is rather towards passivity, a tendency to avoid outside conflicts and struggles rather than to engage in them, a tendency to deal inside the soul with everything that concerns the soul.

In this possibility lies the central problematic of this type of novel: the disappearance of epic symbolisation, the disintegration of form in a nebulous and unstructured sequence of moods and reflections about moods, the replacement of a sensuously meaningful story by psychological analysis. This problematic is further intensified by the fact that, given the relationship between the two, the outside world which comes into contact with such an interiority has to be completely atomised or amorphous, and in any case must be entirely devoid of meaning. It is a world entirely dominated by convention, the full realisation of the concept of a 'second nature'; a quintessence of meaningless laws in which no relation to the soul can be found. And this means that all formal objectivations of social life lose all significance for the soul. They do not retain even their paradoxical significance as being the necessary arena and vehicle of events whilst having no essence at the core. Thus, a character's profession loses all importance from the point of view of his inner destiny, just as marriage, family and class become immaterial to the relationships between characters. Don Quixote would be unthinkable as anything other than a knight, but the story of his love is unimaginable without the troubadours' convention of adoration of the woman; in *The Human Comedy*, the demonic obsession of all the characters is concentrated and objectified in the structures of social life; in Pontoppidan's novel, even though the social structures are unmasked as inessential for the soul, it is nevertheless the struggle concerning them—the recognition of their inessentiality and the effort to reject them—that fills the

hero's life and the novel's action. In the type of novel which
we are now considering, all the relationships have ceased
to exist from the start. The elevation of interiority to the
status of a completely independent world is not only a
psychological fact but also a decisive value judgement
on reality; this self-sufficiency of the subjective self is
its most desperate self-defence; it is the abandonment of
any struggle to realise the soul in the outside world, a
struggle which is seen *a priori* as hopeless and merely
humiliating.

This attitude is so intensely lyrical that it is no longer
capable of purely lyrical expression. Lyrical subjectivity has
to go for its symbols to the outside world; even if that world
has been made by subjectivity itself, it is nevertheless the
only possible one; subjectivity, as an interiority, never confronts in a polemical or negative way the outside world that
is co-ordinated to it, it never takes refuge inside itself in
an effort to forget the outside world; rather, it proceeds as
an arbitrary conqueror, it snatches fragments out of the
atomised chaos which is the outside world and melts them
down—causing all origins to be forgotten—into a newly
created, lyrical cosmos of pure interiority. Epic interiority,
by contrast, is always reflexive, it realises itself in a conscious,
distantiated way in contrast to the naïve distancelessness of
true lyricism. Therefore its means of expression are secondary
ones—mood and reflexion—which, despite some apparent
similarities to those of pure lyricism, have nothing whatever
to do with the essence of the latter. Reflexion and mood
are constitutive structural elements of the novel form, but
their formal significance is determined precisely by the fact
that the regulative system of ideas on which the whole reality
is based can manifest itself in them and is given form through
their mediation; in other words, by the fact that they have
a positive, although problematical and paradoxical, relationship to the outside world. When they become an end in

themselves, their unpoetic and form-destructive character becomes clearly obvious.

This aesthetic problem, however, is at root an ethical one, and its artistic solution therefore presupposes, in accordance with the formal laws of the novel, that a solution has been found to the ethical problem. The hierarchical question of whether inner reality is superior to outer reality or vice versa is the ethical problem of utopia: the question whether the ability to imagine a better world can be ethically justified, and the question whether this ability can serve as the starting point for a life that is rounded in itself, not one which, as Hamann says, has been stopped by having a hole put in it instead of coming to an end. From the point of view of epic form the problem can be posed as follows: can this rounded correction of reality be translated into actions which, regardless of outward failure or success, prove the individual's right to self-sufficiency—actions which do not compromise the mental attitude from which they sprang? To create, by purely artistic means, a reality which corresponds to this dream world, or at least is more adequate to it than the existing one, is only an illusory solution. The utopian longing of the soul is a legitimate desire, worthy of being the centre of a world, only if it is absolutely incapable of being satisfied in the present intellectual state of man, that is to say incapable of being satisfied in any world that can be imagined and given form, whether past, present or mythical. If a world can be found that satisfies the longing, this only proves that the dissatisfaction with the present was merely an artistic quibbling over its outward forms, an aesthetic hankering after times when the artist could draw with more generous lines or paint with brighter colours than today. Such longings can indeed be satisfied, but their inner emptiness becomes apparent in the work's lack of idea, as is, for instance, the case with Walter Scott's novels, well-told though they are.

The flight from the present is of no use whatever in solving the central difficulty. The same problems—often giving rise to a profound dissonance between behaviour and soul, between outward destiny and inner fate—are evident in distantiated works, whether monumental or decorative. *Salammbô* or C. F. Meyer's novels (which are, it is true, designed as novellas) are characteristic examples of this. The aesthetic problem, the transformation of mood and reflexion, of lyricism and psychology into genuinely epic means of expression is therefore centred on the fundamental ethical problem—the question of necessary and possible action. The human type of the central character in works of this kind is in essence a contemplative rather than an active one, and so the epic representation of such a type is faced with the problem of how his rhapsodically retiring or hesitant behaviour can be translated into action; the artistic task consists of revealing the point at which such a character's *being-there* and *being-thus* coincides with his inevitable failure.

The completely pre-determined nature of this failure is the other objective difficulty of purely epic form-giving. The danger of a subjectively lyrical attitude towards events, instead of a normatively epic attitude of absorption and reproduction, is much greater when fatality is predetermined —whether this fatality is affirmed or negated, lamented or scorned—than when the outcome of the struggle has not been decided in advance. The mood which carries and nourishes such lyricism is the mood of disillusioned romanticism, an over-intensified, over-determined desire for an ideal life as opposed to the real one, a desperate recognition of the fact that this desire is doomed to remain unsatisfied, a utopia based from the start on an uneasy conscience and the certainty of defeat. And the decisive feature of this certainty is its inseparable connection with moral conscience, the evidence that failure is a necessary consequence of its own inner structure, that it is, in its finest essence and highest value, condemned to death. That is why the attitude both towards the hero and towards the outside world is a lyrical one, compounded of love and accusation, of sorrow, pity and scorn.

The inner importance of the individual has reached its historical apogee: the individual is no longer significant as the carrier of transcendent worlds, as he was in abstract idealism, he now carries his value exclusively within himself; indeed, the values of being seem to draw the justification of their validity only from the fact of having been subjectively experienced, from their significance to the individual's soul.

> *Si l'arche est vide où tu pensais trouver la loi,*
> *Rien n'est réel que ta danse :*
> *Puisqu'elle n'a pas d'objet, elle est impérissable.*
> *Danse pour le désert et danse pour l'espace.*
>
> Henri Franck.

The precondition and the price of this immoderate elevation of the subject is, however, the abandonment of any claim to participation in the shaping of the outside world. The romanticism of disillusionment not only followed abstract idealism in time and history, it was also conceptually its heir, the next historico-philosophical step in *a priori* utopianism. There, the individual, the vehicle of the utopian challenge to reality, was crushed by the brute force of reality; here, defeat is the precondition of subjectivity. There, subjectivity gave rise to the heroism of militant interiority; here, a man can become the hero, the central figure of a literary work, because he has the inner possibility of experiencing life as a literary creator. There, the outside world was to be created anew on the model of ideals; here, an interiority which perfects itself in the form of a literary work demands from the outside world that is should provide it with suitable material for thus forming itself. In Romanticism, the literary nature of the *a priori* status of the soul vis-à-vis reality becomes conscious: the self, cut off from transcendence, recognises itself as the source of the ideal reality, and, as a necessary consequence, as the only material worthy of self-realisation. Life becomes a work of literature; but, as a result, man becomes the author of his own life and at the same time the observer of that life as a created work of art. Such duality can only be given form by lyrical means. As soon as it is fitted into a coherent totality, the certainty of failure becomes manifest; the romanticism becomes sceptical, disappointed and cruel towards itself and the world; the novel of the Romantic sense of life is the novel of disillusionment. An interiority denied the possibility of fulfilling itself in action turns inwards, yet cannot finally renounce what it has lost forever; even if it wanted to do so, life would deny it such a satisfaction; life forces it to continue the struggle and to suffer defeats which the artist anticipates and the hero apprehends.

This situation gives rise to a romantic lack of moderation in all directions. The inner wealth of pure soul-experience is seen immoderately as the only essential thing; the futility of the soul's existence in the totality of the world is exposed with an equally immoderate ruthlessness; the soul's loneliness, its lack of any support or tie, is intensified until it becomes immeasurable, and, at the same time, the cause of this condition of the soul in a specific world situation is mercilessly revealed. Compositionally speaking, a maximum of continuity is aimed at, since existence is possible only within a subjectivity that is uninterrupted by any outside factor or event; yet reality disintegrates into a series of mutually absolutely heterogeneous fragments which have no independent valency of existence even in isolation, as do the adventures of Don Quixote. All the fragments live only by the grace of the mood in which they are experienced, but the totality reveals the nothingness of this mood in terms of reflexion. And so everything has to be denied, for any affirmation will destroy the precarious balance of forces: affirmation of the outside world would justify the mindless philistines who accommodate themselves to reality, and the resulting work would be no more than cheap, slick satire; straightforward affirmation of romantic interiority would give rise to form-less wallowing in vain, self-worshipping lyrical psychologism. But the outside world and the interiority are too hetero-geneous, too hostile to one another to be simultaneously affirmed, as can happen in novels that overlap into the epic. The only way left is to deny them both, and this merely renews and potentiates the fundamental danger of this type of novel—that of the form becoming dissolved in dreary pessimism. The purely artistic consequences of such a situation are inevitably, on the one hand, the dis-integration of all secure and unconditional human values and the revelation of their ultimate nullity, and, on the other hand, the overall dominance of mood, that is to say of im-potent sorrow over a world which is inessential in itself and which has only the ineffective, monotonous brilliance of a surface in process of decomposition.

Any form must contain some positive element in order to acquire substance as a form. The paradoxical nature of the novel is most strikingly revealed in the fact that the world situation and the human type which most closely corres-pond to its formal requirements—for which it is the only adequate form—confront the writer with almost insoluble problems. Jacobsen's novel of disillusionment, which expresses in wonderful lyrical images the author's melancholy over a world 'in which there's so much that is senselessly exquisite', breaks down and disintegrates completely; and the author's attempt to find a desperate positiveness in Niels Lyhne's heroic atheism, his courageous acceptance of his necessary loneliness, strikes us as an aid brought in from outside the actual work. This hero's life which was meant to become a work of literature and is instead only a poor fragment, is actually transformed into a pile of débris by the form-giving process; the cruelty of disillusionment devalues the lyricism of the moods, but it cannot endow the characters and events with substance or with the gravity of existence. The novel remains a beautiful yet unreal mixture of voluptuousness and bitterness, sorrow and scorn, but not a unity; a series of images and aspects, but not a life totality.

Goncharov's attempt to fit the magnificently, truly and profoundly seen character of Oblomov into a totality by introducing a positive counter-figure was likewise doomed to failure. The memorable recurring image of Oblomov lying on his bed—an image which forcefully and sensually conveys the passivity of this type of character—cannot save the work as a whole. In face of the depth of Oblomov's tragedy—Oblomov whose innermost experience is so direct and bears so exclusively on essential things, yet who has to fail so abysmally whenever he is confronted with the smallest manifestation of outward reality—in face of this the triumphant happiness of Stolz, his 'strong' friend, becomes trivial and flat. At the same time, Stolz has just enough real strength and weight to reduce Oblomov's fate to pettiness; the terrifying comic quality of the divorce between interior and exterior, symbolised by Oblomov lying on his bed, increasingly loses its created depth and greatness as the real action of the novel proceeds—namely, Stolz's attempt to re-educate Oblomov and the failure of that attempt. Oblomov's tragi-comic destiny is increasingly reduced to the indifferent fate of a character doomed to failure from the start.

The greatest discrepancy between idea and reality is time: the process of time as duration. The most profound and most humiliating impotence of subjectivity consists not so much in its hopeless struggle against the lack of idea in social forms and their human representatives, as in the fact that it cannot resist the sluggish, yet constant progress of time; that it must slip down, slowly yet inexorably, from the peaks it has laboriously scaled; that time—that ungraspable, invisibly moving substance—gradually robs subjectivity of all its possessions and imperceptibly forces alien contents into it. That is why only the novel, the literary form of the trans-cendent homelessness of the idea, includes real time— Bergson's *durée*—among its constitutive principles. In an-other context[1] I have pointed out that the drama does not know the concept of time: it is subject to the three unities and, provided these are properly understood, the unity of time signifies a state of being lifted out of the duration of time. The epic, it is true, appears to allow for the duration of time—we need only think of the ten years of the Iliad or of the Odyssey. Yet this time has as little reality, as little real duration, as time has in drama; men and destinies re-main untouched by it; it has a dynamic of its own, and its function is solely to express the greatness of an enterprise or of a tension in a meaningful way. The years are necessary to make the listener understand the real meaning of the capture of Troy and the wanderings of Odysseus, just as the large number of warriors or the vast areas travelled are necessary for the same purpose. But the heroes do not experi-ence time within the work itself; time does not affect their inner changes or changelessness; their age is assimilated in their characters, and Nestor is old just as Helen is beautiful or Agamemnon mighty. It is true that the characters of the epic know life's painful lesson of growing old and dying, but

---

[1] *A modern drama fejlödésének története* (History of the Development of Modern Drama), 2 vols., Budapest 1912. The introductory chapter is available in German under the title *Zur Soziologie des modernen Dramas* in: *Archiv für Sozialwissenschaften und Sozialpolitik* XXXVII (1914), p. 303 ff., p. 662 ff.

to them it is mere knowledge, mere recognition; what they experience and the way they experience it has the blissful time-removed quality of the world of gods. The normative attitude towards the epic, according to Goethe and Schiller, is an attitude assumed towards something completely in the past; therefore its time is static and can be taken in at a single glance. The author of an epic and his characters can move freely in any direction inside it; like all space, it has several dimensions but no direction. And the normative present tense of the drama, likewise laid down by Goethe and Schiller, transforms time into space (as Gurnemanz says). Only the complete disorientedness of modern literature poses the impossible task of representing development and the gradual passing of time in dramatic terms.

Time can become constitutive only when the bond with the transcendental home has been severed. Just as ecstasy elevates the mystic into a sphere where all duration and all passing of time have ceased and from which he must fall back into the world of time only because of his creaturely, organic limitations, so any close and visible connection with the essence creates a cosmos which is *a priori* exempt from this necessity. Only in the novel, whose very matter is seeking and failing to find the essence, is time posited together with the form: time is the resistance of the organic—which possesses a mere semblance of life—to the present meaning, the will of life to remain within its own completely enclosed immanence. In the epic the life-immanence of meaning is so strong that it abolishes time: life enters eternity as life, the organic retains nothing of time except the phase of blossoming; fading and dying are forgotten and left entirely behind. In the novel, meaning is separated from life, and hence the essential from the temporal; we might almost say that the entire inner action of the novel is nothing but a struggle against the power of time.

In the Romanticism of disillusionment, time is the corrupting principle: poetry, the essential, must die, and time is ultimately responsible for its passing. That is why in such novels all value is on the side of the defeated protagonist, who, because he is dying, is endowed with the beauty of wounded youth, while coarseness, harshness, the absence of an idea, belong entirely to time. Only as a post-facto correction of this one-sided lyrical opposition to the victorious power does self-irony turn against the dying essence by endowing it, negatively, with the attributes of youth; the ideal is said to be constitutive only for the soul in a state of immaturity. The overall design of the novel is bound to be deformed if positive and negative values are so distinctly divided between the two sides of the struggle. A form cannot really deny a life principle unless it is capable of excluding it *a priori* from its realm; as soon as it has to admit that principle, it must admit it as positive; and so this principle, not only as an opposing force but in its own right, becomes a precondition of the realisation of value.

Time is the fullness of life, although the fullness of time is the self-abolition of life and, with it, of time itself. The positive thing, the affirmation which the very form of the novel expresses no matter how inconsolably sad its content may be, is not only that distant meaning which dawns with a mild radiance on the far side of the search and the failure to find, but also the fullness of life which is revealed precisely through the manifold failures of the struggle and search. The novel is the form of mature virility: its song of comfort rings out of the dawning recognition that traces or lost meaning are to be found everywhere; that the enemy comes from the same lost home as the knight and defender of the essence; that life had to lose its immanence of meaning so that it might be equally present everywhere.

Thus it is that time becomes the carrier of the sublime

epic poetry of the novel: it has become inexorably existent, and no one can any longer swim against the unmistakable direction of its current nor regulate its unforeseeable course with the dams of *a priori* concepts. Yet a feeling of resignation persists: all this had to come from somewhere, must be going somewhere; even if the direction betrays no meaning, it is a direction none the less. From this feeling of resignation mixed with courage there spring experiences of time which are authentically epic because they give rise to action and stem from action: the experiences of hope and memory; experiences of time which are victories over time: a synoptic vision of time as solidified unity *ante rem* and its synoptic comprehension *post rem. In re*, there can be no simple, happy experience of this form or of the times which have produced it. Experiences of this kind can only be subjective and reflexive; nevertheless there is always in them the form-giving sense of *comprehending a meaning*; they are experiences in which we come as near as we can, in a world forsaken by God, to the essence of things.

Such an experience of time is the basis of Flaubert's *L'Education sentimentale*, and the absence of such an experience, a one-sidedly negative view of time, is what has ultimately been responsible for the failure of the other major novels of disillusionment. Of all great works of this type, *L'Education sentimentale* appears to be the least composed; no attempt is made here to counteract the disintegration of outside reality into heterogeneous, brittle and fragmentary parts by some process of unification or to replace absent connections or valencies of meaning by lyrical mood-imagery: the separate fragments of reality lie before us in all their hardness, brokenness and isolation. The central figure is not made significant by means of limiting the number of characters, by the rigorous convergence of the composition upon the centre, or by any emphasis upon the central character's outstanding personality: the hero's inner life is as fragmentary as the outside world, his interiority possesses no lyrical power of scorn or pathos that might set it against the pettiness of reality. Yet this novel, of all novels of the nineteenth century, is one of the most typical of the problematic of the novel form; in the unmitigated desolation of its matter it is the only novel that attains true epic objectivity and, through it, the positiveness and affirmative energy of an accomplished form.

This victory is rendered possible by time. The unrestricted, uninterrupted flow of time is the unifying principle of the homogeneity that rubs the sharp edges off each heterogeneous fragment and establishes a relationship—albeit an irrational and inexpressible one—between them. Time brings order into the chaos of men's lives and gives it the semblance of a spontaneously flowering, organic entity; characters having no apparent meaning appear, establish relations with one another, break them off, disappear again without any meaning having been revealed. But the characters are not simply dropped into that meaningless becoming and dissolving which preceded man and will outlast him. Beyond events, beyond psychology, time gives them the essential quality of their existence: however accidental the appearance of a character may be in pragmatic and psychological terms, it emerges from an existent, experienced continuity, and the atmosphere of thus being borne upon the unique and unrepeatable stream of life cancels out the accidental nature of their experiences and the isolated nature of the events recounted.

The life totality which carries all men here becomes a living and dynamic thing: the expanse of time which the novel covers, dividing men into generations and integrating their actions in a historico-social context, is not an abstract concept, not a unit conceptually constructed after the event like that of the totality of the *Comédie humaine*, but a thing existing in itself and for itself, a concrete and organic continuum. This totality is a true image of life in the sense that no value-system of ideas enters it except in a regulative function; the only idea immanently contained within it is that of its own existence, that of life as such. But this idea, which reveals more brutally than anything else how infinitely remote we are from the true systems of ideas that have become ideals in the minds of men, at the same time makes the failure of all endeavours seem less desolate. Everything that happens may be meaningless, fragmentary and sad, but it is always irradiated by hope or memory. And hope here is not an abstract artifact, isolated from life, spoilt and shop-worn as the result of its defeat by life: it is a part of life; it tries to conquer life by embracing and adorning it, yet is repulsed by life again and again. And memory trans-forms the continual struggle into a process which is full of mystery and interest and yet is tied with indestructible threads to the present, the unexplained instant. Duration ad-vances upon that instant and passes on, but the wealth of duration which the instant momentarily dams and holds still in a flash of conscious contemplation is such that it enriches even what is over and done with: it even puts the full value of lived experience on events which, at the time, passed by unnoticed. And so, by a strange and melancholy paradox, the moment of failure is the moment of value; the compre-hending and experiencing of life's refusals is the source from which the fullness of life seems to flow. What is depicted is the total absence of any fulfilment of meaning, yet the work attains the rich and rounded fullness of a true totality of life.

Herein lies the essentially epic quality of memory. In the drama (and the epic) the past either does not exist or is completely present. Because these forms know nothing of the passage of time, they allow of no qualitative difference between the experiencing of past and present; time has no power of transformation, it neither intensifies nor diminishes the meaning of anything. This is the formal meaning of the typical scenes of revelation and recognition which Aristotle shows us; something that was pragmatically unknown to the heroes of the drama enters their field of vision and, in the world thus altered, they have to act otherwise than they might wish to act. But the force of the newly introduced factor is not diminshed by a time perspective, it is absolutely homogeneous with and equivalent to the present. Similarly, the passage of time alters nothing in the epic. In adapting the Song of the Nibelungs, Hebbel was able to take over without change Kriemhild's and Hagen's inability to forget—the precondition of their revenge—because such an inability belongs essentially to drama. In the *Divine Comedy*, the remembered earthly life of each character is as present to their souls as is Dante, to whom they are speaking, or as is the actual place of their punishment or reward. As for lyric poetry, change alone is essential for any lyrical experience of the past; lyric poetry knows no object, structured as such, that might exist either in the vacuum of timelessness or in the atmosphere of passing time: it gives form to the process of remembering or forgetting, and the object is only a pretext for lived experience.

Only in the novel and in certain epic forms resembling the novel does memory occur as a creative force affecting the object and transforming it. The genuinely epic quality of such memory is the affirmative experience of the life process. The duality of interiority and the outside world can be abolished for the subject if he (the subject) glimpses the organic unity of his whole life through the process by which his living present has grown from the stream of his past life dammed up within his memory. The surmounting of duality—that is to say the successful mastering and integration of the object—makes this experience into an element of authentically epic form.

The mood-conditioned pseudo-lyricism of the novel of disillusionment betrays itself most obviously by the fact that subject and object are sharply separated in the experience of remembering; memory, from the viewpoint of present subjectivity, grasps the discrepancy between the object as it was in reality and the subject's ideal image of it. The harsh and depressing quality of such works is therefore due not so much to the intrinsically sad nature of the content as to the unresolved dissonance of the form—to the fact that the object of experience is constructed in accordance with the formal laws of drama, whereas the experiencing subject is a lyrical one.

Drama, lyric poetry and the epic, whatever the hierarchy in which we may place them, are not the thesis, antithesis and synthesis of a dialectical process; each of them is a means, qualitatively quite heterogenous from the others, of giving form to the world. Each form appears positive because it fulfils its own structural laws: the affirmation of life that seems to emanate from it as a mood is nothing other than the resolving of its form-conditioned dissonances, the affirmation of its own, form-created substance.

The objective structure of the world of the novel shows a heterogeneous totality, regulated only by regulative ideas, whose meaning is prescribed but not given. That is why the unity of the personality and the world—a unity which is dimly sensed through memory, yet which once was part of our lived experience—that is why this unity in its subjectively constitutive, objectively reflexive essence is the most profound and authentic means of accomplishing the totality required by the novel form. The subject's return home to itself is to be found in this experience, just as the anticipation of this return and the desire for it lie at the root of the experience of hope. It is this return home that, in retrospect, completes everything that was begun, interrupted and allowed to fall by the way—completes it and turns it into rounded action. The lyrical character of moods is transcended in the mood of experiencing this homecoming because it is related to the outside world, to the totality of life. And the insight which grasps this unity, because it is thus related to the object, rises above mere analysis; it becomes an intuitive, premonitory comprehension of the unattained and therefore inexpressible meaning of life—the innermost core of all action made manifest.

A natural consequence of the paradoxical nature of this art form is the fact that the really great novels have a tendency to overlap into the epic. *L'Education sentimentale* is the only real exception to this and is therefore best suited to serve as a model of the novel form. The tendency occurs most obviously in the representation of the passage of time and in the relation of time to the artistic centre-point of the entire work. Pontoppidan's *Hans im Glück* (which, of all nineteenth-century novels, comes closest, perhaps, to Flaubert's great achievement) determines the goal, the attaining of which justifies and completes the life totality of the hero, too concretely as to content, with too much emphasis on value, to achieve perfect, genuinely epic unity at the end. For this hero, the journey through life is more than just an inevitable complication of the ideal: it is the necessary detour without which the goal would be empty and abstract and its attainment valueless. But the hero himself has value only in relation to this specific goal, and his value is only that of *having-grown*, not of *growing*. His lived experience of time therefore has a slight tendency to overlap into the dramatic— to separate critically what is sustained by value from what has been abandoned by meaning. Pontoppidan checks this tendency with admirable tact, but its vestiges, as incompletely surmounted dualities, are still present in the work.

Abstract idealism and its intimate relation with the transcendent homeland which lies on the far side of time makes this overlapping of the novel with the epic necessary. That is why the greatest work of this type, *Don Quixote*, overlaps still more obviously into the epic in its formal and historico-philosophical foundations. The events in *Don Quixote* are almost timeless, a motley series of isolated adventures complete in themselves, and while the ending completes the work as a whole as to its principle and problems, it does so only for the whole and not for the concrete totality of the parts. Therein lies the epic quality of *Don Quixote*, its marvellous hard serenity which is outside any atmosphere. Of course it is only the created work itself that reaches beyond the passage of time and into purer regions: the life base which supports the work is neither timeless nor mythical, it belongs to time passing and everything bears the traces of its origin in time. The light of a demonic, irrational faith in a non-existent transcendent homeland absorbs the shadows and reflections of this origin and puts sharp contours round every image. But it cannot make us forget that origin, for the work owes its inimitable blend of wry serenity and powerful melancholy to this unique and unrepeatable victory over the gravity of time. Here as in everything else, it was not Cervantes, the naïve artist, who surmounted the dangers—unsuspected by him—of his chosen form and found the way to an improbable perfection: it was Cervantes the intuitive visionary of the unique historico-philosophical moment. His vision came into being at the watershed of two historical epochs; it recognised and understood them, and raised the most confused problematic into the radiant sphere of a transcendence which achieved its full flowering as *form*.

The formal ancestor and the formal heir of *Don Quixote* —the chivalrous epic and the adventure novel—both demonstrate the danger inherent in this form, the danger which arises from its overlapping into the epic, from its inability to give form to the *durée*: the danger of triviality, of being reduced to mere entertainment. This is the necessary problematic of this type of novel, just as disintegration and formlessness, which are due to a failure to surmount time as a too-heavy, too strongly existent factor, are the dangers inherent in the other novel form, the novel of disillusionment.

3

Wilhelm Meister's Years of Apprenticeship
as an attempted synthesis

Wilhelm Meister stands aesthetically and historico-philo-sophically between these two types of novel. Its theme is the reconciliation of the problematic individual, guided by his lived experience of the ideal, with concrete social reality. This reconciliation cannot and must not be the result of accommo-dation or of a harmony existing from the start which would make it a modern humorous novel (a type we have already described), except that, whereas in such novels the pre-existing harmony is a necessary evil, here it would become the central good. (Freytag's *Soll und Haben* is a classic example of such objectivation of the lack of idea and of the anti-poetic principle.)

The type of personality and the structure of the plot are determined by the necessary condition that a reconciliation between interiority and reality, although problematic, is nevertheless possible; that it has to be sought in hard struggles and dangerous adventures, yet is ultimately possible to achieve. For this reason the interiority depicted in such a novel must also stand between the two previously analysed types: its relation to the transcendent world of ideas is neither subjectively nor objectively very strong; the soul is not purely self-dependent, its world is not a reality which is, or should be, complete in itself and can be opposed to the reality of the outside world as a postulate and a compet-ing power; instead, the soul in such a novel carries within itself, as a sign of its tenuous, but not yet severed link with the transcendental order, a longing for an earthly home which may correspond to its ideal—an ideal which eludes positive definition but is clear enough in negative terms. Such an

interiority represents on the one hand a wider and consequently more adaptable, gentler, more concrete idealism, and,
on the other hand, a widening of the soul which seeks fulfilment in action, in effective dealings with reality, and not
merely in contemplation. It is an interiority which stands half-
way between idealism and Romanticism, and its attempt,
within itself, to synthesise and overcome both of them is
rejected by both as a compromise.

It follows from this possibility, given by the theme itself,
of effective action in social reality, that the organisation of the
outside world into professions, classes, ranks, etc., is of
decisive importance for this particular type of personality as
the substratum of its social activity. The content and goal of
the ideal which animates the personality and determines his
actions is to find responses to the innermost demands of his
soul in the structures of society. This means, at least as a
postulate, that the inherent loneliness of the soul is surmounted; and this in turn presupposes the possibility of human
and interior community among men, of understanding and
common action in respect of the essential. Such community
is not the result of people being naïvely and naturally rooted
in a specific social structure, not of any natural solidarity
of kinship (as in the ancient epics), nor is it a mystical experience of community, a sudden illumination which rejects
the lonely individuality as something ephemeral, static and
sinful; it is achieved by personalities, previously lonely and
confined within their own selves, adapting and accustoming
themselves to one another; it is the fruit of a rich and en-
riching resignation, the crowning of a process of education,
a maturity attained by struggle and effort.

The content of such maturity is an ideal of free humanity
which comprehends and affirms the structures of social life
as necessary forms of human community, yet, at the same
time, only sees them as an occasion for the active expression
of the essential life substance—in other words, which takes

possession of these structures, not in their rigid political and legal being-for-themselves, but as the necessary instruments of aims which go far beyond them. The heroism of abstract idealism and the pure interiority of Romanticism are therefore admitted as relatively justified, but only as tendencies to be surmounted and integrated in the interiorised order; in themselves and for themselves, they appear as reprehensible and doomed to perdition, as also is philistinism—the acceptance of an outside order, however lacking in idea it may be, simply because it is the given order.

This structure of the relationship between the ideal and the soul relativises the hero's central position, which is merely accidental: the hero is picked out of an unlimited number of men who share his aspirations, and is placed at the centre of the narrative only because his seeking and finding reveal the world's totality most clearly. In the tower where Wilhelm Meister's years of apprenticeship are recorded, those of Jarno and Lothario and others—both members and non-members of the League—are recorded too, and the novel itself contains, in the memories of the Canoness, a close parallel to the story of the hero's education. It is true that in the novel of disillusionment, the central character's position is also often accidental (whereas abstract idealism has to make use of a hero marked out and placed at the centre of events by his loneliness); but this is more a means of exposing the corrupting nature of reality: where all interiority is bound to come to grief, any individual destiny is merely an episode, and the world consists of an infinite number of such isolated, mutually heterogeneous episodes which have only the fatality of failure in common. Here, however, the philosophical basis of the relativity of the hero's position is the possibility of success of aspirations aimed at a common goal; the individual characters are closely linked together by this community of destiny, whereas in the novel of disillusionment the parallelism of their lives had only to enhance their loneliness.

This is why Goethe in *Wilhelm Meister* steers a middle course between abstract idealism, which concentrates on pure action, and Romanticism, which interiorises action and reduces it to contemplation. Humanism, the fundamental attitude of this type of work, demands a balance between activity and contemplation, between wanting to mould the world and being purely receptive towards it. This form has been called the 'novel of education'—rightly, because its action has to be a conscious, controlled process aimed at a certain goal: the development of qualities in men which would never blossom without the active intervention of other men and circumstances; whilst the goal thus attained is in itself formative and encouraging to others—is itself a means of education.

A story determined by such a goal has a certain calm based on security. But this is not the calm of an a-prioristic world; the will towards education, a will that is conscious and certain of its aim, is what creates the atmosphere of ultimate security. The world of such a novel in itself and for itself is by no means free from danger. In order to demonstrate the risk which everyone runs and which can be escaped by individual salvation but not by a-prioristic redemption, many characters have to perish because of their inability to adapt themselves, whilst others fade away because of their precipitous and unconditional surrender in the face of reality. Ways towards individual salvation do exist, however, and a whole community of men is seen to arrive successfully at the end of them, helping one another, as well as occasionally falling into error during the process. And what has become a reality for many must be at least potentially accessible to all.

The robust sense of security underlying this type of novel arises, then, from the relativation of its central character, which in turn is determined by a belief in the possibility of common destinies and life-formations. As soon as this belief disappears—which, in formal terms, amounts to saying:

as soon as the action of the novel is constructed out of the destinies of a lonely person who merely passes through various real or illusory communities but whose fate does not finally flow into them—the form of the work must undergo a substantial change, coming closer to that of the novel of disillusionment, in which loneliness is neither accidental nor the fault of the individual, but signifies that the desire for the essence always leads out of the world of social structures and communities and that a community is possible only at the surface of life and can only be based on compromise. The central character becomes problematic, not because of his so-called 'false tendencies', but just because he wants to realise his deepest interiority in the outside world. The educative element which this type of novel still retains and which distinguishes it sharply from the novel of disillusionment is that the hero's ultimate state of resigned loneliness does not signify the total collapse and defilement of all his ideals but a recognition of the discrepancy between the interiority and the world. The hero actively realises this duality: he accommodates himself to society by resigning himself to accept its life forms, and by locking inside himself and keeping entirely to himself the interiority which can only be realised inside the soul. His ultimate arrival expresses the present state of the world but is neither a protest against it nor an affirmation of it, only an understanding and experiencing of it which tries to be fair to both sides and which ascribes the soul's inability to fulfil itself in the world not only to the inessential nature of the world but also to the feebleness of the soul.

In most individual examples the dividing line between this post-Goethean type of novel of education and the novel of disillusionment is often fluid. The first version of *Der Grüne Heinrich* shows this perhaps most clearly, whereas the final version stands definitely upon the course required by its form. But the possibility of such indeterminacy (although it can be overcome) reveals the one great danger inherent in this form because of its historico-philosophical base: the danger of a subjectivity which is not exemplary, which has not become a symbol, and which is bound to destroy the epic form. The hero and his destiny then have no more than personal interest and the work as a whole becomes a private memoir of how a certain person succeeded in coming to terms with his world. (The novel of disillusionment counteracts the increased subjectivity of the characters by the crushing, equalising universality of fate.) Such a subjectivity is even more difficult to surmount than that of the impersonal narrative: it endows everything—even if the technique is perfectly objectivised —with the fatal, irrelevant and petty character of the merely private; it remains a mere aspect, making the absence of a totality the more painfully obvious as it constantly claims to create one. The overwhelming majority of modern 'novels of education' have completely failed to avoid this pitfall.

The structure of the characters and destinies in *Wilhelm Meister* determines the structure of the social world around them. Here, too, we have an intermediate situation: the structures of social life are not modelled on a stable and secure transcendent world, nor are they in themselves an order, complete and clearly articulated, which substantiates itself to become its own purpose; such a world would exclude any possibility of the hero's seeking or losing his way. But neither do these structures form an amorphous mass, for then the interiority oriented towards finding an order would always remain homeless and the attainment of the goal would be unthinkable from the start. The social world must therefore be shown as a world of convention, which is partially open to penetration by living meaning.

A new principle of heterogeneity is thereby introduced into the outside world: a hierarchy of the various structures and layers of structures according to their penetrability by meaning. This hierarchy is irrational and incapable of being rationalised; and the meaning, in this particular case, is not objective but is tantamount to the possibility of a personality fulfilling itself in action. Irony here acquires crucial importance as a factor in the creation of the work because no structure in itself and for itself can be said to possess such meaning, nor not to possess it; it is quite impossible to decide from the start whether any structure is thus eligible or not, and only its interaction with the individual can reveal this. The necessary ambiguity is further increased by the fact that in each separate set of interactions it is impossible to tell whether the adequacy or inadequacy of the structure of the individual is due to the individual's success or failure or whether it is a comment on the structure itself. But such an ironic affirmation of reality—for this uncertainty lights up even a reality totally lacking in idea—is, after all, only an intermediate stage: the completion of the process of education must inevitably idealise and romanticise certain parts of reality and abandon others to prose, as being devoid of meaning.

Yet the author must not abandon his ironic attitude, replacing it by unconditional affirmation, even when describing the eventual homecoming. This objectivation of social life is merely the occasion for something which lies outside and beyond it to become visible, fruitful and active, and the earlier ironic homogeneisation of reality, to which the homecoming owes its character of reality—its nature which always remains opaque to subjective views and tendencies, its independent existence vis-à-vis them—cannot be abolished even at the eventual homecoming without endangering the unity of the whole. And so the attained, meaningful and harmonious world is just as real and has the same characteristics of reality as the different degrees of meaninglessness and of partial penetration by meaning which preceded it in the story.

In this ironic tact of the Romantic presentation of reality lies the other great danger inherent in this form of the novel, which only Goethe—and not always he—succeeded in escaping. It is the danger of romanticising reality to a point where it becomes a sphere totally beyond reality or, still more dangerously from the point of view of artistic form-giving, a sphere completely free from problems, for which the forms of the novel are then no longer sufficient. Novalis, who rejected Goethe's work as prosaic and anti-poetic precisely on these grounds, sets the fairy-tale—transcendence realised in reality—as the goal and canon of epic poetry against the method used in *Wilhelm Meister*. '*Wilhelm Meister's Years of Apprenticeship*,' he writes, 'is in a sense a completely prosaic and modern work. The Romantic element is absent from it, and so is the poetry of nature—the miraculous. It deals only with ordinary, human things; nature and mysticism are quite forgotten. It is a poeticised story of bourgeois domestic life. The miraculous is dismissed from it as mere poetry and exaltation. Artistic atheism is the spirit of this book . . . It is at bottom . . . unpoetic to the highest degree, however poetical the writing may be.' And again, Novalis' own harking back to the age of the chivalrous epics was not accidental but the result of that enigmatic and yet so deeply rational elective affinity between an author's fundamental intention and the matter of his works. Novalis, like the authors of those epics, wanted to create a totality of revealed transcendence within an earthly reality (although we can speak only of an *a priori* sharing of aims, not of any direct or indirect 'influence'). His stylisation, like that of the chivalrous epics, had therefore to be oriented towards the fairy-tale. But whereas the intention of the authors of the medieval epics was epic in a naïvely natural sense and consisted in giving form directly to real life (the glimpsed presence of the transcendent and, with it, the transfiguration of reality into a fairy-tale being merely a gift they received from their historico-philosophical situation), for Novalis this fairy-tale reality as a re-creation of the broken unity between reality and transcendence became a conscious goal. And this is precisely why he could not achieve a decisive and complete synthesis. His reality is so much weighed down by the earthly gravity of idealessness, his transcendent world is so airy, so vapid, because it stems too directly from the philosophico-postulative sphere of pure abstraction, that the two are unable to unite in a living totality. And so the artistic fault which Novalis so penetratingly detected in Goethe is even greater —is irreparable—in his own work.

The triumph of poetry, its transfiguring and redeeming domination of the entire universe, has not the constitutive force to make all earthly and prosaic things follow it into paradise; the romanticising of reality merely gives reality a lyrical semblance of poetry, but this semblance cannot be translated into events—into epic terms; and so the genuinely epic in Novalis' work suffers from the same problematic as in Goethe's (but to a more acute degree) or is evaded alto-gether by lyrical reflexions and mood-pictures. Novalis' stylisation remains a purely reflexive one, superficially dis-guising the danger but in fact only intensifying it. Lyrical, mood-dominated romanticising of the structures of social reality cannot, given the fact that reality at the present stage of development lacks pre-stabilised harmony, relate to the essential life of the interiority. Since Novalis rejected Goethe's solution of seeking an ironical, fluctuating balance maintained from the point of view of the subject and touching as little as possible upon the actual structures of society, no other way was left open to him but to poeticise these structures in their objective existence and to create a world which was beautiful and harmonious but closed within itself and unrelated to anything outside: a world connected only reflexively, only by mood, not in any epic sense, with the ultimate realised transcendence or with the problematic interiority: a world which therefore could not become a true totality.

The surmounting of this danger is not entirely problem-free even in Goethe. Although he places strong emphasis on the merely potential and subjective nature of the penetration of meaning into the social sphere in which the hero finds fulfilment, the notion of community on which the whole edifice is based requires that the social structures should here possess a greater, more objective substantiality and, therefore, a more genuine adequation to the normative subjects, than those spheres which have been overcome.

This objective removal of the fundamental problematic brings the novel closer to the epic; yet it is impossible for a work which began as a novel to end as an epic, and it is likewise impossible, once such overlapping has occurred, to make the work homogeneous again by the renewed use of irony. This is why, in *Wilhelm Meister*, the world of the nobility, which does not belong completely to the novel and so is somewhat fragile, has to be set as a symbol of active life-domination against the marvellously unified atmosphere of the theatre, which is born of the true spirit of the novel form. Certainly, by the nature of the marriages which conclude the novel, the nobility as a social estate is interiorised with the maximum epic and sensuous intensity, so that the objective superiority of a class is transformed to mean a better opportunity for a freer, more generous way of life for anyone possessing the necessary inner potentialities. But in spite of this ironic reservation, a social class is nevertheless raised to a height of substantiality to which it cannot inwardly be equal. Within this class, although confined to a small circle of its members, a universal and all-embracing cultural flowering is supposed to occur, capable of absorbing the most varied individual destinies. In other words, the world thus confined within a single class—the nobility—and based upon it, partakes of the problem-free radiance of the epic.

Not even the supreme artistic tact with which Goethe introduces new problems at this late stage in the novel can alter the immanent consequences of the novel's ending. The world he describes, with its merely relative adequation to essential life, contains no element that can offer a possibility for the necessary stylisation. This is why Goethe was obliged to introduce the much-criticised fantastic apparatus of the last books of the novel, the mysterious tower, the all-knowing initiates with their providential actions, etc. Goethe makes use here of the methods of the (Romantic) epic. He absolutely needed these methods in order to give sensuous significance and gravity to the ending of the novel, and although he tried to rob them of their epic quality by using them lightly and ironically, thus hoping to transform them into elements of the novel form, he failed. With his creative irony, by means of which he was able everywhere else to give substance to things that were in themselves unworthy of artistic treatment and to control any tendency to go beyond the novel form, he devalued the miraculous by revealing its playful, arbitrary and ultimately inessential character. And he could not prevent it from introducing a disrupting dissonance into the total unity of the whole; the miraculous becomes a mystification without hidden meaning, a strongly emphasised narrative element without real importance, a playful ornament without decorative grace. This was more than a concession to the taste of the period (as many have claimed in apology), and after all it is quite impossible to imagine *Wilhelm Meister* without this miraculous element, however inorganic it may be. An essential formal necessity forced Goethe to use it and its use had to fail only because, given the author's fundamental intention, it was oriented towards a less problematic form than that imposed by its substratum —that is to say, the historical epic.

Again, the author's utopian outlook prevents him from stopping at the mere portrayal of the time-given problematic; he cannot be satisfied with a mere glimpse, a merely subjective experience of an unrealisable meaning; he is forced to posit a purely individual experience, which may, postulatively, have universal validity, as the existent and constitutive meaning of reality. But reality refuses to be forced up to such a level of meaning, and, as with all the decisive problems of great literary forms, no artist's skill is great and masterly enough to bridge the abyss.

4

Tolstoy and the attempts to go beyond the social forms of life

THE OVERLAPPING of the novel form into the epic, such as we have discussed, is rooted in social life; it disrupts the immanence of form only to the extent that, at the crucial point, it imputes a substantiality to the world it describes which that world is in no way capable of sustaining and keeping in a state of balance. The artist's epic intention, his desire to arrive at a world beyond the problematic, is aimed only at an immanently utopian ideal of social forms and structures; therefore it does not transcend these forms and structures generally but only their historically given concrete possibilities—and this is enough to destroy the immanence of form.

This attitude appears first in the novel of disillusionment, where the incongruence of interiority and the conventional world leads to a complete denial of the latter. But so long as this denial signifies no more than an inner attitude, the immanence of the novel—provided the form is successfully achieved—remains intact, and any lack of balance is more a question of a lyrical and psychological general disintegration of the form than of an overlapping of the novel into the epic. (We have already analysed the special case of Novalis.) Such overlapping is, however, unavoidable if the utopian rejection of the conventional world objectivises itself in a likewise existent reality, so that polemical refusal actually becomes the central form of the work. No such possibility was given by the historical development of Western Europe.

This utopian demand of the soul is directed at something unattainable from the start—at an outside world which might

144

be adequate to a highly differentiated, refined soul that has become an interiority. The rejection of convention is not aimed at conventionality itself but, in part, at its divorce from the soul and, in part, at its lack of refinement. Its character, which is that of civilisation but not of culture, and its dry and arid lack of spirituality are both rejected. Apart from purely anarchistic tendencies which could almost be called mystical, what is desired is always a culture objectivising itself in structures which might be adequate to the interiority. (This is the point at which Goethe's novel connects with this particular development, except that in *Wilhelm Meister* such a culture is actually found, which gives the book its singular rhythm: layers of social structures, which become more and more essential as the hero matures and gradually discards abstract idealism and utopian Romanticism, increasingly surpass his expectations.) Criticism (rejection) of this kind can only express itself lyrically. Even in Rousseau, whose Romantic world view entailed the refusal of all cultural structures, the polemicism takes the form of pure polemicism, i.e. it is rhetorical, lyrical, reflexive. The world of Western European culture is so deeply rooted in the inescapability of its constituent structures that it can never adopt any attitude towards them other than a polemical one.

The greater closeness of nineteenth-century Russian literature to certain organic natural conditions, which were the given substratum of its underlying attitude and creative intention, made it possible for that literature to be *creatively* polemical. Tolstoy, coming after Turgenev—who was an essentially Western European novelist of disillusionment— created a form of novel which overlaps to the maximum extent into the epic. Tolstoy's great and truly epic mentality, which has little to do with the novel form, aspires to a life based on a community of feeling among simple human beings closely bound to nature, a life which is intimately adapted to the great rhythm of nature, which moves according to nature's cycle of birth and death and excludes all structures which are not natural, which are petty and disruptive, causing disintegration and stagnation. 'The muzhik dies quietly,' Tolstoy wrote to Countess A. A. Tolstoy about his story *Three Deaths*. 'His religion is nature, with which he has spent all his life. He has felled trees, sown rye, reaped it, he has slaughtered sheep and sheep have been born on his farm, children have come into the world, old men have died, and he knows this law from which he has never turned away as the lady of the manor has done, he knows it well and has looked it straight and simply in the eye . . . The tree dies quietly, simply and beautifully. Beautifully because it does not lie, makes no grimaces, is afraid of nothing and regrets nothing.'

The paradoxical nature of Tolstoy's historical situation, which proves better than anything else how much the novel is the necessary epic form of our time, manifests itself in the fact that this world cannot be translated into movement and action, even by an author who not only longs for it but has actually seen and depicted it clearly; it remains only an element of the epic work, but is not epic reality itself. The natural organic world of the old epics was, after all, a culture whose organic character was its specific quality, whereas the nature which Tolstoy posits as the ideal and which he has experienced as existent is, in its innermost essence, meant to be *nature* (and is, therefore, opposed, as such, to *culture*). This necessary opposition is the insoluble problematic of Tolstoy's novels. In other words, his epic intention was bound to result in a problematic novel form, not because he failed to overcome culture within himself, not because his relationship to nature as he experienced and depicted it was a sentimental one—not for psychological reasons—but for reasons of form and of the relationship of form to its historico-philosophical substratum.

A totality of men and events is possible only on the basis of culture, whatever one's attitude towards it. Therefore in Tolstoy's epic works the decisive element belongs, both as framework and as concrete content, to the world of culture which he rejects as problematic. But since nature, although it cannot become an immanently complete totality, is objectively existent, the work contains two layers of realities which are completely heterogeneous from one another both as regards the value attached to them and the quality of their being. And relating them to one another, which would make it possible to construct a work that was a totality, can only take the form of the lived experience of going from one reality to the other. Or, to put it more precisely, since the direction chosen is a given result of the value attached to both realities, it is the experience of going from culture to nature. And so, as a paradoxical consequence of the paradoxical relationship between the writer's mentality and the historical age in which he finds himself, a sentimental, romantic experience finally becomes the centre of the entire work: the central characters' dissatisfaction with whatever the surrounding world of culture can offer them and their seeking and finding of the second, more essential reality of nature. The paradox arising from this experience is further increased by the fact that this 'nature' of Tolstoy's does not have a plenitude and perfection that would make it, like the relatively more substantial world at the end of Goethe's novel, a home in which the characters might arrive and come to rest. Rather, it is a factual assurance that an essential life really does exist beyond conventionality—a life which can be reached through the lived experiences of a full and genuine selfhood, the self-experience of the soul, but from which one must irremediably fall back into the world of convention.

With the heroic ruthlessness of a writer of historic greatness, Tolstoy does not flinch from the grim consequences of

his world view; not even the singular position he allocates to
love and marriage—a position half-way between nature and
culture, at home in both spheres and yet a stranger in each
—can mitigate these consequences. In the rhythm of natural
life, the rhythm of unpathetic, natural growth and death,
love is the point at which the dominant forces of life assume
their most concrete and meaningful form. Yet love as a pure
force of nature, love as passion, does not belong to Tolstoy's
world of nature; passionate love is too much bound up with
the relationship between one individual and another and
therefore isolates too much, creates too many degrees and
nuances; it is too cultural. The love which occupies the really
central place in Tolstoy's world is love as marriage, love
as union (the fact of being united, of becoming one, being
more important than who it is that is thus united), love as
the prelude to birth; marriage and the family as a vehicle
of the natural continuity of life. That this introduces a
conceptual dichotomy into the edifice would be of little
importance artistically if it did not create yet another heterogeneous layer of reality, which cannot be compositionally
connected with the other two spheres, in themselves
heterogeneous from each other. The more authentically this
layer of reality is depicted, the more strongly it is bound to
be transformed into the opposite of what was intended: the
triumph of such love over culture is meant to be a victory
of the natural over the falsely, artificially refined, yet it becomes a miserable swallowing-up by nature of everything that
is great and noble in man. Nature is alive inside man but,
when it is lived as culture, it reduces man to the lowest, most
mindless, most idea-forsaken conventionality. This is why the
mood of the epilogue to *War and Peace*, with its nursery
atmosphere where all passion has been spent and all seeking
ended, is more profoundly disconsolate than the endings of the
most problematic novels of disillusionment. Nothing is left
of what was there before; as the sand of the desert covers the

pyramids, so every spiritual thing has been swamped, annihilated, by animal nature.

This unintentional disconsolateness of the ending combines with an intentional one in the description of the conventional world. Tolstoy's evaluating and rejecting attitude extends to every detail he depicts. The aimlessness and insubstantiality of the life he describes expresses itself not only objectively, for the reader who recognises it, not only as the lived experience of gradual disappointment, but also as an a-prioristic, established, agitated emptiness, a restless *ennui*. Every conversation, every event bears the stamp of the author's verdict.

These two groups of experiences (the private world of marriage and the public world of society) are contrasted with the experience of the essence of nature. At very rare, great moments—generally they are moments of death—a reality reveals itself to man in which he suddenly glimpses and grasps the essence that rules over him and works within him, the meaning of his life. His whole previous life vanishes into nothingness in the face of this experience; all its conflicts, all the sufferings, torments and confusions caused by them, appear petty and inessential. Meaning has made its appearance and the paths into living life are open to the soul. And here again Tolstoy, with the paradoxical ruthlessness of true genius, shows up the profoundly problematic nature of his form and its foundations: these crucial moments of bliss are the great moments of dying—the experience of Andrey Bolkonsky lying mortally wounded on the field of Austerlitz, the sense of unity experienced by Karenin and Vronsky at Anna's deathbed—and it would be true bliss to die now, to die like that. But Anna recovers and Andrey returns to life, and the great moments vanish without trace. Life goes on in the world of convention, an aimless, inessential life. The paths which the great moments had revealed lose their direction, their reality, as the great moment passes. Such paths cannot be trodden, and when people believe they are treading them, their experience is a bitter caricature of what the revelation of the great moment had shown. (Levin's experience of God and his clinging to what he has thus attained—despite the fact that it is slipping from his grasp—stems more from the will and theory of Tolstoy the thinker than from the vision of Tolstoy the artist. It is programmatic and lacks the immediate conviction of the other great moments.) The few characters who are capable of really living their lived experiences—perhaps Planton Karatayev is the only such character—are, of necessity, secondary characters: events leave them unchanged, their essential nature is never involved in events, their life does not objectivise itself, it cannot be given form but only hinted at, only defined in concrete artistic terms in contrast to the others. They are not realities but marginal aesthetic concepts.

These three layers of reality correspond to the three concepts of time in Tolstoy's world, and the impossibility of uniting them reveals most strongly the inner problematic of his works, rich and profound as they are. The world of convention is essentially timeless; an eternally recurring, self-repeating monotony, it proceeds upon its course in accordance with meaningless laws of its own; eternal movement without direction, without growth, without death. Characters come and go, but nothing happens as a result of this constant flux because each figure is as insubstantial as the next, and any one can be put in the place of any other. Whenever one walks on to this stage, whenever one leaves it, one always finds—or has to reject—the same motley inessentiality. Beneath it flows the stream of Tolstoyan nature: the continuity and monotony of an eternal rhythm. That which changes in nature is the individual destiny, and this, too, is inessential. Individual destiny, caught in the current, rising or sinking with it, possesses no meaning founded upon itself; its relation to the whole does not assimilate its personality but destroys it; as an individual destiny, rather than as an element of a general rhythm side by side with innumerable other, similar and equivalent lives, it is completely immaterial. The great moments which offer a glimpse of an essential life, a meaningful process, remain mere moments, isolated from the other two worlds and without constitutive reference to them. Thus the three concepts of time are not only mutually heterogeneous and incapable of being united with one another, but moreover none of them expresses real duration, real time, the life-element of the novel.

Going outside and beyond culture has merely destroyed culture but has not put a truer, more essential life in its place; the overlapping into the epic only makes the novel form still more problematic, without coming concretely closer to the desired goal, the problem-free reality of the epic. (In purely artistic terms Tolstoy's novels are novels of disillusionment carried to an extreme, a baroque version of Flaubert's form.) The glimpsed world of essential nature remains an intimation, a lived experience; it is subjective and reflexive so far as the depicted reality is concerned; but in a purely artistic sense, it is nevertheless of the same kind as any other longing for a more adequate reality.

Literary development has not yet gone beyond the novel of disillusionment, and the most recent literature reveals no possibility of creating another type that would be essentially new; what we have now is an eclectic, epigonic imitation of earlier types, whose apparent productive force is confined to the formally inessential areas of lyricism and psychology.

Tolstoy himself, it is true, occupies a dual position. From the point of view purely of form (a point of view which, in Tolstoy's special case, cannot possibly do justice to what matters most in his vision or in his created world), he must be seen as the final expression of European Romanticism. However, in the few overwhelmingly great moments of his works—moments which must be seen as subjective and reflexive in respect of each particular work as a whole—he shows a clearly differentiated, concrete and existent world, which, if it could spread out into a totality, would be completely inaccessible to the categories of the novel and would require a new form of artistic creation: the form of the renewed epic.

This world is the sphere of pure soul-reality in which man exists as man, neither as a social being nor as an isolated, unique, pure and therefore abstract interiority. If ever this world should come into being as something natural and simply experienced, as the only true reality, a new complete totality could be built out of all its substances and relationships. It would be a world to which our divided reality would be a mere backdrop, a world which would have outstripped our dual world of social reality by as much as we have outstripped the world of nature. But art can never be the agent of such a transformation: the great epic is a form bound to the historical moment, and any attempt to depict the utopian as existent can only end in destroying the form, not in creating reality. The novel is the form of the epoch of absolute sinfulness, as Fichte said, and it must remain the dominant form so long as the world is ruled by the same stars. In Tolstoy, intimations of a breakthrough into a new epoch are visible; but they remain polemical, nostalgic and abstract.

It is in the words of Dostoevsky that this new world, remote from any struggle against what actually exists, is drawn for the first time simply as a seen reality. That is why he, and the form he created, lie outside the scope of this book. Dostoevsky did not write novels, and the creative vision revealed in his works has nothing to do, either as affirmation or as rejection, with European nineteenth-century Romanticism or with the many, likewise Romantic, reactions against it. He belongs to the new world. Only formal analysis of his works can show whether he is already the Homer or the Dante of that world or whether he merely supplies the songs which, together with the songs of other forerunners, later artists will one day weave into a great unity: whether he is merely a beginning or already a completion. It will then be the task of historico-philosophical interpretation to decide whether we are really about to leave the age of absolute sinfulness or whether the new has no other herald but our hopes: those hopes which are signs of a world to come, still so weak that it can easily be crushed by the sterile power of the merely existent.

Index of Names

Index of Subjects